The Corporate Climbing Game

By Nick Kelso

Illustrations by James Hunt

First published 2020

ISBN

Front cover design; Linda Verhorevoort

To Katie, Michael,
and their descendants

About the author

Nick Kelso was born in Nigeria in 1962, and spent his childhood in both the UK, and the Netherlands. He was educated at Brockenhurst College and Lancaster University where he read Philosophy and History. He is author of Errors of Judgement, (Hale 1988) The Alpine Game (2007), The Freefall Game (2008) and currently works for a Multinational company as a corporate social entrepreneur looking to improve primary care facilities across Africa. In 2000, he emigrated to the Netherlands, where he still lives with his wife Dimphy and his daughter Katie.

Contents

Foreword

Mountaineering and adventure can really inspire people, support a healthy lifestyle and help organisations achieve their objectives. These simple insights are the underlying theme of this autobiography.

By this I do not mean an international bank sponsoring a major 'last problem' climbing expedition, or those so called 'team building' days out with the department when staff go on an outdoors course, build a basic if rickety bridge across a stream or something like that and have a drink and meal together afterwards.

I mean instead that employees and partner organizations can be inspired, brought together and bond, create new ideas, and solve problems or promote solutions, by being set the multi-day challenge of climbing a *real* mountain or undergoing a *real* adventure together.

In the modern corporation, this can touch upon human resources, sales & marketing, corporate brand & corporate social-responsibility programmes, management teams, innovation and research. These pages record my own experiences in this niche field and this book is a follow up to 'The Alpine Game' an earlier autobiographical account, which I wrote in 2007. This highlighted the sense of personal achievement and camaraderie, which stems from shared adventures.

Here is an example. In 2011 I made a proposal to my management team to organize a week long boot camp for thirteen young so called 'high potential' employees from our then Africa team. The mixed team, mainly from Egypt, Morocco and South Africa, were tasked with creating a new business plan for our Africa business with new ideas. We could have gone to a local hotel somewhere and locked ourselves away for five days, but I saw it as an opportunity for an experiment.

What if we took the team to Zermatt for the week and rented self-catering apartments with views of the Matterhorn? And what if, in addition, we created a program too acclimatize and prepare the group, in between and after their working sessions, for a team ascent of the Breithorn (4164 m) at the end of the week?

Would this combination of inspiring surroundings, a relaxed but tough working regime and a seemingly impossible challenge/shared experience, create exciting new ideas? (Remember, from Zermatt the north face of the Breithorn looks rather imposing to the un-initiated).

I did not know the answer either, but submitted a proposal along these lines. It was accepted and the results were both positive and surprising.

In this respect I have always remembered a training I attended in the late 1980s, in London, when I was told; "There is always someone who can say '*yes*' to your plans and ideas. You just need to find this person"

This has indeed proved excellent advice.

My motivation in recording these stories, many of which take place in Africa is not merely to highlight a new 'controlled risk taking niche genre in marketing'.

I want to inspire my children and their descendants to find their own games to play in life, to make their lives more meaningful, healthy and less susceptible to stalling in the face of the inevitable tough challenges they might meet.

At the end of 'The Alpine Game', I had written 'I will not stop visiting the Alps. I simply love the challenges, the places, the people, the views and the history; in short the whole experience'.

This is still the key. Whatever the future brings and for as long as I can, I simply want to express the joy of life and the inspiration that mountaineering and adventure has given to me, and many of those around me.

Nick Kelso

The Netherlands 2017

"Are you the person who can say 'yes' to my big idea?"

If you want to go fast – go alone

If you want to go far – go together

Old African saying

1. 'The Highest Siblings on the Planet' 2007-2008

I do not remember exactly when I had the simple idea of combining my love of mountaineering and adventure with my work, as a communications manager in one of the divisions of a multinational corporation in the southern Netherlands. It had certainly happened by early 2007. That January I stood up in front of our marketing and business teams and invited them to come and climb Kilimanjaro with me.

I stressed three key points; namely that we would be promoting our own business solutions to climate change; that we would be raising money for a charity and finally that, we would be experiencing the magnificent challenge of climbing the highest mountain in Africa.

The ground rules were also made clear. We would do this at our own expense and in our own time as this had to come from the heart. In making this offer I felt on relatively safe ground, having climbed Kilimanjaro twice before in 1990 and 2005 and knowing the guiding and porter support that we would have.

What I was not prepared for was the reaction.

It was as if a dam of conformity had burst open and the excitement was palpable. Within days, some forty-five people had signed up for the challenge, including many very senior managers, and we quickly closed the offer.

It was a heady time. My sister Annetta and another work colleague called Marius and I, set up a steering group and allocated ourselves different tasks. They were the practical ones, checking flights, costs and a whole host of other things. My tasks involved mostly smiling and talking.

Many other co-workers and friends expressed their full support, but explained they would have to be there in spirit only, as disabilities, finances and family ties were in the way.

A few weeks later, we had organized ourselves. We would raise money for a water project in Tanzania run by Oxfam Novib, and appropriately, at the bottom of the slopes overlooking Kilimanjaro itself. We had quotes for air travel and had decided on our dates. 'Let's go late December and come back early January. That way we could have New Year's Eve on the mountain'.

We had worked on a communications plan to promote a switch to energy efficient lighting which had a name 'Save the Snow'. This was a clear reference to the disappearing snows on the summit of Kilimanjaro.

However, we also had the climbing part to engage us. I briefed the forty-four others in detailed sessions on such mechanics as required fitness-levels, clothing and equipment, and advised them all to check with their doctors to see if they could make the trip. I also described the route and showed photos. We would be taking the Rongai route and traversing the mountain in six days, from the Kenyan side down to the main gates at Marangu. I had arranged for us to be fully supported and guided, by a trekking company based in Nairobi – Kibo Slopes Safaris – who I knew well.

'And you really need to listen to your guide', I heard myself saying. However, I saved what I hoped would be the most inspiring story to last.

The maxim 'thinking outside the box' is a commonplace one today and I applied it to the world of mountains. I started by asking them, which was the highest mountain in the world, to which the answer was 'Everest of course'. I then went on to point out that, there were in fact at least three ways to measure the height of a mountain. It is only when determined from sea level that the answer is Everest.

A second way is to measure a mountain from its bottom to its top, and then the highest in the world is one of the Hawaiian

15

volcanoes, more than 95% of which is under water. A third way is to measure from the centre of the earth to the bit of the world that sticks furthest into space, and here the answer is Chimborazo in Ecuador at 6268 metres. This is because the earth is not completely round, but bulges outwards at the equator due to the centrifugal force arising from its rotation; a phenomenon that 'distorts' heights by more than three km. It also means incidentally that Ecuador's Cotopaxi is a big player in the 'real' height stakes.

This much was well known and published but now I introduced my own analysis. The nearest mountain to the equator in Africa is Kilimanjaro at 5895 metres. This was not as high as Chimborazo but that did not necessarily matter I claimed due to the time difference between Ecuador and Tanzania. When you have reached the summit of Kilimanjaro at around 0800 in the morning, it will be around midnight in South America, thus unlikely that anyone would be around on the top three hundred and fifty metres of Chimborazo at that time (or any other nearby Andean peak).

Therefore, and, with my tongue firmly in my cheek, I suggested that there was a good chance that when we stood on top of Kilimanjaro in the early morning, we would at that moment be sticking out further into space than anyone else on the surface of the planet. Or put another way we might well be 'the highest people on the planet'.

Of course, we were unlikely to ever really *know,* which made the idea more intriguing. There were many smiles after this and I have no doubt many private claims have since been made !

It was very pleasing that Annetta had joined the group. Having given birth to three sons in rapid succession, she now clearly needed a little break of her own. Two years younger than me, we had worked at the same company together for twenty years and

could easily share ideas on the planning. In addition, I knew that
if we both made it, our claim to be the highest siblings on the
planet would probably survive anyone topping out on
Chimborazo in South America at the same time!

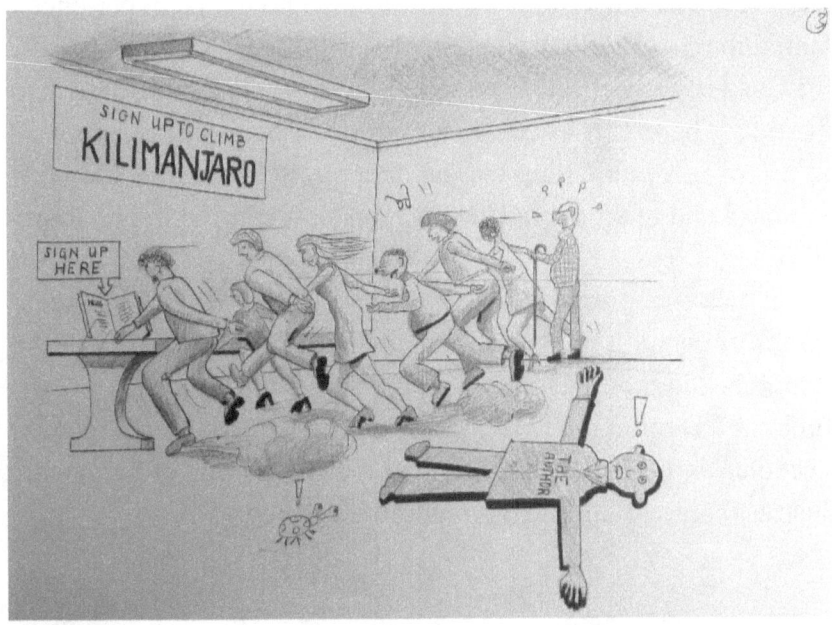

"So, who wants to climb Kilimanjaro with me?"

That spring and early summer, I prepared for my own Alpine
trip. This has been described in the last chapter of 'The Alpine
Game' so no repeat is needed here, except to say that it turned
out to be an excellent two weeks climbing which included
ascents of the Monch and the Jungfrau in testing conditions. It
was at the end of this holiday in early August 2007, that I
decided to record my own experiences as at best a very average
Joe Alpinist, with no pretensions to any great skills, but having
nevertheless a tremendous passion for the Alps.
Initially, I had no other idea than leaving an account for my

friends and family, and hopefully future grandchildren. Back in the mid to late 1980s my first book, on SOE's disaster in the Netherlands during the Second World War had been at the mercy of publishers and agents. It had seemed like a closed shop industry, frustratingly slow, unrewarding and not an experience I wanted to repeat.

Nor was I writing for money, given my well-paid employment situation. Therefore, I was more than interested to learn about the rise of self-publishing via the internet. Suddenly I could be in control and make all the key decisions; it spurred me on in my efforts.

It took me three months to write and complete the book – three months of evening time and weekends, in which I poured out the memories and thoughts of almost a quarter of century of climbing adventures. Friends chipped in with proof reading and anecdotes and James Hunt provided some excellent drawings to illustrate some of our most memorable moments!

I was reasonably happy with the result, which for all its faults managed to capture my own feelings and the atmosphere at the time as I recalled it. I remember a friend once questioning my memory on some aspect or other, then bursting out in laughter, after seeing my face, saying "I know – write your own book then eh'" Auto-biographical works are subjective things!

All of this effort meant that by the time I came up for air in November 2007 – the big trip was nearly upon us. I had not managed much training but still cycled to work and back for an hour every day, and had managed to lose some weight. As I had performed well in the Alps just a few months previously, I felt reasonably confident of my own fitness, although conscious that many eyes would be watching me in the coming weeks.

In the meantime our 'Save the Snow', fundraising had gone extremely well. Between us, we had raised about hundred thousand US dollars for Oxfam-Novib, which included a large donation from our own CEO. Our publicity had spread widely across the internet, and been picked up by the local Dutch media, who were keen to follow the story. We had even compensated our carbon footprint, mostly our flights, by buying and installing the latest energy saving light bulbs.

We now totaled forty-six people, as we added one more to the list once we realized that we could cope with an even number in the tents.

Kibo Slopes Safaris had asked us to split ourselves into teams of about fifteen, in order to manage us better. In effect, we would be three connected, but independent groups. These were based on an International group speaking English, a father/sons and family group and a young couples group , the last two being Dutch speaking. We named these 'Kibo', 'Mawenzi', and 'Uhuru' and managed to accommodate all the personal requests connected. Annetta and I were in Kibo and this was the international team, with seven different nationalities.

The other two were mostly Dutch. Messages of support came from all corners, including from Sir Bob Geldof and the Dutch Prime Minister Jan-Peter Balkenende, who wished us good luck. Spirits were high as Christmas approached.

The Dutch economy, indeed the world economy, had been booming for a while, with house prices going up; money easy to borrow and jobs seemingly secure. Many people felt relaxed about life. Looking back now it was an almost unreal period, where the natural laws of economics did not seem to matter. Domestically we had weathered the 'Katie arrival' of a few years earlier and our beautiful daughter was now six years old and growing quickly. She spoke English, Dutch and Polish fluently and we were busy integrating her at a local Dutch primary school. Her brother, Michael, was by now living and working in Dublin, and on his own steep learning curve in life.

One place that was not doing quite so well was Kenya, our initial destination. With spectacular bad timing, we managed to arrive in Nairobi on the very morning after the general elections. Within days, tribal politics would turn violent, and some fifteen-hundred people were murdered. Up to another six hundred thousand would become homeless, transforming the country from a friendly tourist destination to gruesome, front-page global news. Because this was happening whilst we were on the mountain and in Tanzania at the time, we were probably some of the last people on the planet to hear about it. However, we were due to return via Nairobi, and as we later found out, this was to cause some considerable consternation back in Europe.

We landed in the Kenyan capital after a night flight, and were collected in an efficient and friendly way by the Kibo Slopes Safaris team with six vehicles. Everything seemed normal at the time, and that evening we were at a lodge near the Tanzanian border. We crossed the border in the morning and met the Oxfam Novib team, whose water project we had supported. This was called the TIP project (Traditional irrigation project) and involved the construction of irrigation canals around Kilimanjaro itself.
The aim was to focus on 'poverty alleviation' through economic empowerment of smallholding farmers; more water, more crops, more income. We were energized to hear about the project in real life and it was a relief that the hard work that had gone into raising the money had paid off. With so many stories abounding of development money not reaching its target, we had deliberately chosen a reliable Non-Governmental organisation to work with. Later the General Director of Oxfam-Novib wrote us a very kind thank you letter.

The following day we travelled to a lodge near Naromoru at the very start of the Rongai route. It was here, the following morning, that we met our guides and porters. We had also been getting to know each other better. Climbing experience was sparse.

"Some people are saying they have never even slept in a tent before" I was told.

On hearing this, I began to wonder what I had started, but they were all keen and no one was obviously unfit for the work ahead. We had taken many precautions – there were nurses and doctors amongst the group, along with oxygen and even a mobile compression chamber!

There were so many remarkable people. One couple, Roel and his wife Dionne, were medical doctors and were going to carry out their own tests on oxygen saturation. I was surprised to learn that my own blithe assumption, that as you got higher there was less oxygen in the air, was not correct.

Apparently, there is 21% oxygen at sea level, and there is still same percentage in the air at the top of Kilimanjaro. What in fact happens is that as you get higher the pressure of the air gets lower, and hence thinner, allowing the body to process less oxygen into the blood.

Back in the Netherlands, at sea level an oxygen saturation level in the blood of less than 90% would mean that you would be on an additional oxygen supply in a hospital. Roel, Dionne, and their two children were going to measure their own blood oxygen levels, and those of volunteers, all the way up the mountain.

It was going to be fun to hear their findings.

Another couple, Jacky and Larry, another sister and brother combination, were both in their fifties. They were always laughing and smiling about something or other and their humour and love of life was infectious. Yet they held a grim secret, which I have to say we were not aware of at the time. Jacky was terminally ill, and had an expected six months left to live. She was using this time to make her final dream of climbing Kilimanjaro come true, and although aware she might not make the summit, she was determined to enjoy what little time she had left.

Larry was there to support her. I should point out that she did not look at all ill and was a strong walker. They would provide within a few days one of the most poignant moments of the trip, about which more later.

Some of the other characters have already appeared in my stories before. Roger and his son James, now aged sixteen were with us again after their Kilimanjaro attempt in 2005. So too was Marek and his daughter Karolina, with whom we had climbed Mt. Kenya in 2006.

There was Jane, one of the most extraordinary women I have ever come across. Global traveler, natural entrepreneur and owner of a successful communications agency in London do not really begin to describe her.

A great sense of humour, a capacity to think differently and a thousand and one fascinating stories does not either. Jane was an experienced Africa traveler. Sometime in the early 1990's she and a female companion had spent a year travelling, walking mainly, very 'rough and low budget' across West and Central Africa to Kenya.

They had lived 'on the edge' for a long time and, at several stages, it did not look like Jane would survive. She did, mainly I think because of her great mental strength.

Jane had not trained much for the climb. She had no expectations nor even felt any great need to summit. The journey was its own reward. She was a tower of strength and common sense throughout. Her luggage had failed to arrive on

22

time from London, and she started out on the mountain with borrowed kit. It did not finally arrive until we reached camp three! She actually laughed more about it than we did.

I cannot go on without mentioning young Enoch. He was a young Tanzanian, whom I had first met on Kilimanjaro as a porter in 2005.

He was a bright young lad, hardworking and uncomplaining, and as he spoke good English, we had had long chats with him during our descent. We asked him about his life and hopes for the future. He had confided that he wanted to be a safari driver and guide, but lacked the funds to go through the two-year training program.

On our return to Europe in 2005, we had talked about Enoch's situation and how we might help him. We did not want to give him money, but decided we would be willing to club together and pay the fees for the two-year training course. So we had contacted Enoch and got the details of the college he needed to attend.

I remember him ringing me to say thanks, and insisting I talk to his mother, who spoke no English, but whose strong emotions came across very clearly. Enoch had also emailed to say that if I were ever in the area again, he would come and help. I had not forgotten this, and let him know we would be around and hoped he could find time to join us. However, it was not until we met up again at the start of the trek, that I really came to understand the impact of what we had done.

Enoch had been waiting when we arrived and came straight over and gave Roger, Marek and myself a big hug. He then said he would act as my personal porter and would be going to the summit with me – something he had never done before in all the years he had worked on the mountain.

One of his friends confided in me, that in the last year after having finished his training and becoming a driver/guide, he had "become a big man in his village". Enoch incidentally was small and wiry and still only in his early twenties. He would become both a fine companion and fascinating source of local information on the trek ahead.

These were just a few examples of the group who set off for the walk up to Camp 1. Before doing so, we lined up for a group photo and I made a renewed appeal to all of us, to listen to our guides and follow what they said.

We were all naturally concerned with the potential for altitude sickness, and there had been quite a lot of discussion on whether to take Diamox or not. My choice was not too. However, that evening I had cause to remember my own words. At our first camp both Jane and I had planned to bivi outside that night until the chief guide advised us not to. His argument was 'wild animals', but his word was enough.

The first two days passed without incident. We started from Naromoru at around 2000 m and spent our first night in tents, including our mess tents, at about 2800 m. Here Roel and Dionne measured blood oxygen saturation levels of 93% in their group.

Evenings in our 'Kibo' mess tent at least for the first few nights, were always lively and fun. There was Garrett, Irish to the core, always leading the conversation with wit and insight. Roy and Karsten, Norwegian and Danish respectively, who added pithy comments, whilst Marek and his daughter Karolina provided many funny stories.

There was Klaas who was Dutch, a senior research scientist, with a passion for adventure and the outdoors. He always had a huge grin on his face and was probably the strongest, fittest member of our 'Save the Snower's'.

I always felt he was the only one of us who would have stood a chance of climbing Kili solo and unsupported.

On Day 2 we worked our way up to the Kikelewa camp at 3600

m; a long day this one, split by lunch at the caves of the same name. The three groups walked separately, meeting up occasionally at break stops, and there was plenty of talking at this stage.

We passed through the various zones where farmland, thick vegetation, rain forest and heather followed each other, which make climbing the mountain such a pleasant experience. What was immediately noticeable was the team-working element. People started looking out for each other, comparing notes and encouraging each other.

That night, at the Kikelewa camp, we celebrated New Year. The chefs had outdone themselves with fish and chips and other unlikely things, given our location. However a number of us, including myself, missed out due to a sudden attack of 'stomach troubles'.

Starting 2008 in the toilet hut had not been part of the plan, but at least I managed to get some sleep that night and felt somewhat better when I awoke. Annetta, with whom I was sharing a tent throughout, filled me in on events the following morning.

She was having no altitude problems, kept up a cheery banter, and was clearly enjoying herself immensely. Incidentally, Roel and Dionne's oxygen measurements now showed most people below 90%.

On Day 3, the first problem cases started to become apparent. It was only a short walk, but we were going up to Mawenzi tarn hut at 4330 m and the altitude mattered. Anyone who has visited this site will remember its stark beauty – with its beautiful tarn and the backdrop of Mawenzi.

However, as usual, stark beauty in itself is not a cure for a body that has started to protest. The next morning Roger and James decided to descend, as James was being sick. This was a repeat of what had happened in 2005 and I felt for Roger. However, he took it philosophically and was naturally concerned about his son's wellbeing. He was doing the right thing. So too was Marek who had the same problem with daughter Karolina. We said our goodbyes and would meet them in a few days again.

It was also at Mawenzi tarn that we faced our first real issue. There had been some misunderstandings in communication in one of the groups, and there was some question about how well water was being boiled. Some of the guides felt insulted and were not happy.

This needed tackling immediately, so I invited those concerned to a 'clear the air' session in one of the mess tents.

Working on instinct, I started by saying that we were very happy with the guiding and porter support we were getting, and apologised on behalf of the group for any misunderstandings on that score. I then explained why some people had been genuinely worried.

We discussed how we could solve the issue, which had arisen because fifteen people got through a lot of water very quickly. We finished on a positive note with smiles and laughter, and then discussed the plans for the next day and summit push. If we could just hold it together for the next thirty-six hours, I reasoned that nobody would be talking about boiled water. After handshakes all round, I crawled off to my tent with stomach cramps and did not reappear until dinnertime.

In reality, this was an isolated incident, in what was to prove a very happy trip, but I was now starting to worry about how fit I would be for the summit bid.

My own personal aim was to stand on top with Annetta and be 'the highest brother and sister on the planet' but this was starting to look improbable. The oxygen saturation measuring team that afternoon found an average of around 85%.

Our fourth day on the mountain was the toughest yet, although the weather mercifully remained good, as it had been all week. We were now forty-two clients, plus guides and porters and we laboured slowly across a desolate lunar landscape, up to the school hut at 4750 m.

I had worried about this before, as some people would have to camp out, due to numbers, even if only for a few hours, but in the end, there were more than enough volunteers to do this. This was the day I started to recover, and early that evening I had a chat with many people from the other groups, to encourage and tell them what to expect.

Some thirty-eight of us would be setting out on summit day, with four wisely having decided they had gone far enough. Although I had experienced this situation many times before, I now felt responsible in a way I had never done before. Accidents and heart attacks would not only have consequences for the people concerned, but also on my career and employability!

Watching the people in our 'Kibo team' was interesting. They all looked determined and were still laughing and instinctively looking after each other, often in very small ways. Looking back, I am convinced this removed stress levels to such a degree, that it enabled people of average fitness to achieve great things in the next twelve hours.

Roel and Dionne had diligently kept up their work measuring oxygen saturation levels, and many people were already below 80% and that with 1200 m of height gain to go. Perhaps it is better not to know these things on a high mountain!

The lights went out about 19.30 and at 23.15, our short rest was over; the decisive moment had arrived.

Things felt very tense. All around me people were getting up and gathering round the hut table. It was still Wednesday 2 January 2008 and I knew that within thirty minutes, thirty-eight people would be setting out into the dark for the long climb towards the summit. It was the key moment we had worked towards for many months, and I continued to feel a sense of concern. Of course, we were being guided, but all these friends and colleagues were here because I had told them they could do it. Therefore, I felt a strong sense of responsibility for what was going to happen.

As far as I could see, we had covered all the basics. The weather remained fair; we were reasonably acclimatized well fed and supported by our guides. We had the right equipment; had a doctor and nurse with us, and carried an oxygen bottle and mobile decompression chamber.

Surely, nothing could go wrong. I knew that if it did, if we lost one person to oedema or to an unexpected heart attack, the whole project might finish in disaster.

Seven hours later, we stood on the first summit; called Gilman's Point at 5681 m. Confusion reigned as people slapped each other on the back and jostled to take photos on the tiny summit. My rough count showed twenty-two people had made it, out of the first two groups, 'Kibo' and 'Uhuru' - Only a few had dropped out, including unfortunately Jacky, the only one from our group. We had kept up a steady pace and after a few hours, she had dropped back.

Larry at first hung back with her but she had urged him to go on. A guide, and we had three per group - something I had insisted upon, remained with Jacky, but I did not expect to see her again until we were back down.

Our group had otherwise stayed together throughout, constantly encouraging each other along the way. Annetta experienced some tough times in the middle of the night, but after a spectacular sunrise, she had rallied and pushed on. I noted with interest that a number of people whom I had privately not expected would make it, had also kept going and were now smiling before the cameras.

28

Now at Gilman's point, situated on the rim of the summit crater, there were no reports of major problems, although everyone looked tired. The third group 'Mawenzi' was still somewhere below the first summit - They were another fourteen people. Enoch was following my every step. This was also his first ascent.

The guides conferred and we organized ourselves for the next stage. Of the twenty-two at Gilman's, some fifteen decided to go on, including Annetta, Jane and myself. Just two more hours for the family photos, I thought.

Things were looking positive as the first two groups set off for the main Uhuru summit, another two hours away. This was a crucial stage, as there is no easy retreat from here in case of trouble. The route follows the crater rim around to its highest point, and once on it you are committed with no quick way down.

There was little talking now as we plodded onwards. We rounded Stella Point and could now see the finishing line.

I took the lead and raced together with Marius towards the summit post. As we got closer, we could see that there was no snow at all left in the summit area. So much for 'Save the Snow'!

We had in fact passed some patches of white on the way up but compared with 1990 and even 2005, it had all gone. Marius and I linked arms and symbolically stepped up to the new wooden board which now indicates you are at the summit of Africa, at Uhuru peak 5895 m. Elation and fatigue was mixed with pride and other emotions.

Annetta was there, so were Jane, Garrett, Roy, Karsten, Klaas, Arnold from our 'Kibo' team, and all the others from the 'Uhuru' team, who had set off from Gilman's point.

Enoch had made it too but was clearly suffering from the altitude. Despite years of work on the mountain as a porter, he had never been this high before and his body was not adapting. I gave him water and chocolate, a hug, and we took a few photos before I asked him to go down. He initially refused but then relented.

His commitment had been total and he suffered because of it, but I knew that, having summited would stand him in good stead in his future work as a safari guide.

A most unusual photo shoot followed, as people lined up with banners, and our two youngest companions put on the polar bear costumes, which we had brought with us to make our statements to the world. (We had a GSM network connection at the summit) We also had a company flag with us. This had been to the top of Everest, and which on pain of death, we had to bring back! I mentally ran through the number and confirmed we were fifteen at Uhuru and twenty-two at Gilman's.

This left the fourteen from the 'Mawenzi' team, of whom there was still no sign. We lingered for what seemed like a long time - more than half an hour, before people started to descend back to Gilman's point. In that time, Annetta and I captured our own brother and sister moment for posterity.

We were amongst the last to leave the summit and had only gone ten minutes, when we met up with the 'Mawenzi' team still heading doggedly towards the summit with their guides.

Eleven of them had made Gillman's Point and seven of them had continued towards Uhuru. They looked as if they were in another world, as exhaustion had really taken hold.

I told them I would wait at Gillman's Point for them. A quick mental note – twenty-two on top of Africa, with thirty-four at Gilman's, was mixed with concern. They were the last people on the mountain. It was late morning and if anything happened now we would be in trouble.

"Just the two polar bears for now. Right camera lights …
ACTION!"

The Mawenzi team did finally summit, and I remember one
story by Marc who was climbing with his girlfriend Esther. "I
was planning to propose to Esther on the summit" he said "but
then I looked at her and she appeared so unwell I decided not
to." Instead, he waited a week until they were on the beach in
Mombasa! She said "yes".

Back at Gilman's Point, we there was another update. 'Jacky
made it after all……..it is unbelievable…..you should have seen
her reunion with Larry. Her guide sang her to the summit'.

Jacky it now transpired had not gone down after dropping back,
but had continued up at her own pace, accompanied by one of
the most remarkable guides I ever met.

This was fantastic news and someone even showed me the
digital photos and film taken of the reunion. The emotion of that
moment was impossible to put in words. It was palpable for us,

who did not then know of Jacky's illness. For Jacky and Larry, it was both a celebration of her life, her final wish fulfilled and the start of the process of saying goodbye. It put our own sibling moment in perspective.

Jacky's guide sang her to the summit

Meanwhile Roel was one of those who had decided to stay at Gilman's Point. He had the energy to measure his blood oxygen level and recorded a level of 76%. Given that Uhuru peak – the main summit was 200m higher and a mile away, I suspect some of us may have had levels of around 70% by the time we got there. Again, it was probably better not to know!
Everyone was accounted except the seven still out towards Uhuru. A number of us waited for about an hour before they started to come back in. They moved like zombies, but I knew the fact they had summited would give them an extra boost.

Finally they were all back in. As we descended together, the tension drained away from me. The normal rule of climbing a mountain is that the summit is only half way and that getting down is often harder than getting up. This does not really apply on the standard route of Kilimanjaro, which you can just run down.

The rest of the day was a blur of adrenaline-fueled hugs, laughter, bleary-eyed smiles and banter, as we collected first at the Kibo hut, and then descended to the Horombo hut at 3800 m. As usual, summit day had been an eighteen-hour marathon, but success brings its own energy. The mess tents were sparsely attended that night as we all caught up on sleep.

The following day we walked down the standard Mandara route through the beautiful tropical forest. It soon became a free for all with groups fragmenting and people going at their own pace. Often derided as the Coca Cola route, the first half up of the Mandara trail is as beautiful and interesting as anything the mountain has to offer. It also made a nice backdrop to collect my thoughts.

I was intrigued how so many of our 'Kibo' group had made the main summit. Of the original sixteen and allowing for the four who had gone down early, eight had made Uhuru and the other four (Marina, Robert, Jacky & Larry) Gilman's Point. They were not conventionally very fit, some were overweight and virtually none of them had climbing experience, or had been to great altitude before.

Yet there it was; they had not only made it to almost 6000 m, but had been in control and had enjoyed the experience. Before we set out for the summit bid, I had thought privately that if we got half our group to Gilman's Point we would have done well. Why so wrong?

An ascent on this scale was new for me. Until now, my own experience of mountaineering was either solo or with small teams of two to four people. These small teams had been contained and supported each other, but then we were close friends, who trusted each other implicitly. On the 'Save the Snow' trip, it would have been stretching this analogy to describe us all as close friends, despite the fact that we all got on well together.

It was also clear that our group was mentally strong. We were entrepreneurs, business managers of varying level of seniority and, in general, high achievers with an elevated pain threshold. This was no doubt a factor. I also noticed that all the very senior managers had made it. Yet I sensed there was more to it.

Annetta had already noticed it. There had been a great deal of mutual support, warmth, and humour during the past five days. We had experienced no additional stress from petty quarrels or differences, and competitive behaviour had been absent. It was as if we had all instinctively realized that by sticking together in every sense, we would increase our chances.

It then dawned on me, as I idled down the rain forest path, that the key dynamic had been teamwork. This much-used phrase is usually a hope and desire, more than a reality, something to aim for.

Yet I now understood that we had just experienced the real thing. Our species evolved to work in teams, appropriately enough it seems in Africa.

The counter question I asked myself was 'how many of us would have made it up Kilimanjaro alone or just ourselves and a guide?' Maybe a few, but not many and not me, I mused. In addition, these thoughts led me to the bigger picture, namely our superb Tanzanian guides and porters who had made the whole thing possible.

I would hazard to say that only a fraction of those who have ever climbed Kilimanjaro would have succeeded without the support of the porters and guides. Our own teamwork, which was mainly psychological, would itself still have counted for little without the hard work they put in. Rucksacks and supplies carried, tents erected, food and water provided. Moreover, this was great teamwork too.

We had all gotten on well together and felt a deep sense of respect for, and confidence in, our guides and porters.

The end of the trail at Marangu gate did not look or feel much different to when I had last been there in 1990.

By mid-afternoon, everyone had drifted in, including Jacky who had a permanent grin on her face despite looking drained and pale. We now said our goodbyes and thanks to the guides and porters. We had followed the standard advised amounts for tips, but the real bonus was the equipment we left. A lot of our personal gear was donated to the porters.

We also said goodbye to Enoch. He had fully recovered from his altitude problems, and had told me a good deal about his life and about Tanzanian life in general. It was striking how most Africans lived on the front line of life - all the time. Basic illnesses could kill; poverty was endemic of course, and life was tough and often short.

Yet despite this, most people we came across were smiling and laughing. It was hard not to feel respect for, and indeed be moved by, such an attitude to life.

We re-crossed the border into Kenya and stayed at a lodge on the edge of the Amboseli Park. Here we heard for the first time about the horrendous violence that had followed the Kenyan general election. Messages from home started to flood in, where friends and family were concerned about our welfare and our return travel.

At one stage, things had looked so bleak that we understood our CEO had been considering sending a jet to bring us back. In the end, the advice we received from many quarters was that it would be OK to travel back via Nairobi, as the military and police had things under control.

The following day was our last full day in Africa. However, whilst people were going out on safaris I had set myself another task to perform, which looking back was to become more significant for me than our 'Save the Snow' project itself. Before leaving the Netherlands I had collected two of our new solar-powered lights, which I had promised to get some research-feedback on.

According to the World Bank, some five hundred million Africans lack access to electricity and spend many hours each day in the dark, with little access to lighting. With the evenings and nights being long all year round – it goes dark by 19.00 or earlier every day, and the main light source is unhealthy, expensive kerosene lanterns.

My company had developed a new clean and sustainable answer and had asked me to see if I could get some additional research backed as well by feedback when I was in Kenya.

A number of us visited a local Masai community and the impact of the solar lights was immediate. The excitement they created triggered my own interest, and I could suddenly see all kinds of opportunities.

A 'solar-powered light bulb' went on in my own head that day. Clearly, the need was there. Surely, we could improve lives and enable economic progress.

I personally was in the 'help provide the means, rather than the charity handouts school' of thought. Although I did not then know, it was a crucial meeting, which would shape my working life for the next decade and lead to more 'corporate mountaineering projects'.

We travelled back to Nairobi in a concentrated frame of mind. Things were very quiet, the streets mostly deserted, and we reached the airport without incident. Fortunately, the advice we had followed was sound.

Back in the Netherlands, amidst a good deal of support and publicity, many of us were on natural highs for months afterwards. The messages we had sought to highlight about sustainability and energy efficient lighting had been spread widely.

Our story was told in boardrooms; work place coffee corners and in homes all across the Southern Netherlands. For me the main lesson was, that when you worked well together, you were likely to achieve more than, if you did not. It sounds so simple!

Looking back now on our 'Save the Snow' trip, it is now clear that it was a turning point in my life. My desire to help improve life in Africa, in a sustainable way, would become a strong passion, a driving force.

It would also lead to more 'corporate risk-taking' in the coming decade.

The years that followed would be incredibly rewarding, but they would also come at a price.

Above: Our 'Save the Snow' team came from many Nations. We are just about to start the first days climb up to Camp 1

Below: Meeting Enoch again. Education not handouts had widened his opportunities considerably.

Above: Trekking to our high camp on Kilimanjaro. We could not have done this without our porters and guides.

Below: Annetta resting during our night climb to Uhuru peak.

Above: Team Uhuru on the summit of Africa. There was mobile phone coverage and we were able to send messages.

Below: Our 'highest brother and sister' moment. .

Above: Collecting snow samples from near the summit. This was symbolic.

Below: Coming down the interminable scree slope was a lot faster than going up.

Above: Meeting Oxfam representatives. We had raised one hundred thousand USD for a water project in Tanzania.

Below: The start of a new passion – solar powered LED lighting

2. Africa rising. 2008-2009

Life quickly reverted to 'normal' after we got home. I managed to get myself transferred to our Africa Division, which was managed mainly from the Netherlands. Seen by some as an uninteresting backwater, this had proved somewhat easier than I expected.

A vacancy for a communications manager had arisen, and I had quickly secured the job. This was a significant step in the right direction. Even better news was that I was to manage a sizable budget. What we needed were ideas, plans and focus.

We also tried to decide what to do with our samples of Kilimanjaro snow. On the way down, we had collected samples of the snow, now water, in small test tubes, which we had brought along. In the end, we failed this test, being unable to think of any real practical use!

Sadly, some three months after our return from Tanzania, a group of us attended Jacky's funeral. There had been no last minute miracle and I suspect that climbing Kilimanjaro had significantly reduced the time she had left.

However, I also knew she had lived, as she had wanted to during our week together. She had followed her dream and made it happen. I remember a very fine woman.

Work became busy. Late spring, my company signed an agreement to test solar powered lanterns in Africa and I travelled to Egypt and South Africa, talking to people and gaining more knowledge and insights. For several years, there had been a general global perception around that Africa; commercially speaking was a difficult case.

The evidence however was beginning to tell a different story, with economic growth and more competence in management. The era of the psychopathic dictators was mostly over.

That summer in 2008, we went on a family trip to the Alps. Ever since she had been born, I had been waiting to climb an easy Alpine peak with my daughter Katie, then aged seven. A week in Zermatt offered opportunities.

Our friends Richard, Ana Maria and their sons, Alexander aged six and Andreas aged four, would also be going, Mark, and his girlfriend Pamela joined too. We hired apartments in early August and spent the week walking, rock climbing and ascending some modest Alpine peaks. I had hoped to take Katie up the Breithorn, but a stolen wallet meant I had to spend a key-acclimatization day at the bank, and she therefore missed her opportunity.

I had also been busy that summer, writing another book called 'The Freefall Game'. It continued my 'passions that enhance life' philosophy, and was a record of my skydiving adventures between the years 1981-91. During this time I had completed two hundred and eighteen skydives and had many stories to tell. Looking back, I had come to realize that for many years, I had been addicted to adrenaline, and this was the key theme of the book.

Again, I was writing for family, friends and all future offspring. Some instinct told me that it was now or never, as my memory would inevitably fade.

That autumn the economic crisis broke and the world changed forever. Before this, progress and universal prosperity had seemed inevitable. Although the world was full of risks, it was possible to maintain a rosy view of the future, in which by now the first smart phones had arrived.

After 2008, I think that many people began to realize that history might not be one upward line of development, and that our children might, by modern western standards, actually be poorer than we were. I felt fortunate to have grown up with very little and knew that enjoyment of life, particularly if you embraced

44

the outdoors, was not dependent on a lot of money. Friends and family were much more important. One of the consequences soon became several rounds of re-organization, as they were called at my work.

It was during this time I also met up with Roger. He had been to Kilimanjaro twice now, and each time had had to descend to look after his son. This might have dampened his enthusiasm for a third attempt, but he was made of sterner stuff, and in a moment of enthusiasm, I had offered to go with him on the proviso that we did a new route.
We planned to go in the summer of 2009 for a quick nine-day trip, and I started to look around for more people to go with.

A number of friends travelled to Normandy for a weekend, which had become another regular feature in our lives. Back in 2000 we had by chance, gone on a battlefield tour in France. In the years that followed, we had done some more with guides, until I realized that I could do it too.
This led me in 2005, to offer my friends a Battle of Arnhem tour in the Netherlands. I knew the history well and it was quite easy to develop a tour. I should mention that historical reading has been a passion of mine for more than forty years. Since childhood, I had developed an ability for speed-reading, and by now had read literally thousands of books on World War 2, via either libraries or my own growing collection.
About fifteen people came on the tour and a new annual tradition started.
In 2006, we visited Normandy for the story of D-day and in 2007, we went to Monte Casino in Italy, where my brother Will and I did the tour jointly, and now in 2008 we were back in Normandy.
The feedback was very positive, and this encouraged me to think about setting up a small guiding-business as a weekend hobby.

One of the nice things about those trips was that a number of fathers came along and we found this good for generational bonding.

Another activity I undertook during this period, at least once per year, was skiing. I was a late starter, having waited until my late thirties, (never having had the money before) and had then taught myself to ski from scratch in a week.

During the past ten years, Agata and I had skied in Canada, the USA, France, Germany and Austria, all of which funded by the remains of my UK house sale in 2000.

By 2008 however, the main skiing effort was a long weekend with the lads. This included Simon my brother in law, and Allan another Brit work-colleague and we three would drive to Switzerland from the Netherlands.

Terrence would fly in to Salzburg, where we would pick him up. We would then ski intensely for three days, which was enough for me for another year.

November 2008 saw 'The Freefall Game' ready for publication after another big effort by friends to check the copy. James had done some more drawings, which demonstrated some of the many things that made skydiving, back in 1983 at least, a potentially high-risk activity.

I was pleased with the result and it is still my own personal favorite of the 'game' books.

2009 proved a busy year. I started gathering more and more experience of Africa beyond the tourist trail. In January, together with a Dutch colleague and friend called Kees, I travelled for work across Ghana, Uganda and Kenya.

Many memories remain. Sunsets in traditional African villages; sitting with the village elders by the light of a kerosene lantern; listening to the stories and demonstrating our own solar-powered lights. We talked to local NGOs and aid agencies, our own partners and distributors; government officials and sometimes the media.

On other visits to South Africa, I gained insights into Soweto, its troubled history and the hopes and frustrations of young South Africans. I stayed with Afrikaner families; ate with the Indian community and spent a day with a young Zulu, learning about his culture.

He proudly showed me how he had cut off half of his little finger with a razor blade as an initiation ceremony! His mother had been very upset by this, he confessed cheerfully.

Everywhere I was welcomed as an outsider, with whom people could speak openly. There were still many tensions below the surface and I gained even more respect for what Nelson Mandela had ultimately achieved.

Another time in Morocco, I spent four days in a hotel without electricity. By day two, the buffet-food had run out and by the final day, we were eating very stale sandwiches. Yet the people remained calm and friendly. They were used to it.

I also experienced the problem side of the continent. The crime and corruption, the sexual violence and harassment of women, the death rates on the roads, disease and illness, and I was struck early on by the small number of older people that seemed to be around.

Two conclusions were clear.

Firstly, a lack of electrical power in general was holding back social and economic development, and there was a lack of lighting in the evening. Electric lighting could provide more security and extend the day.

The second conclusion was that soccer or football was a universal language, which needed no explanation and could be a great help. One example of this; in Northern Ghana I remembered visiting a remote village, which had a generator and one satellite TV for the entire community. They had enough money for kerosene for one big showing per week. What did they watch? A 'live match from the UK premier league'.

I mention all this as background to the first 'big idea' I had for our business.

We had long known that South Africa would host the 2010 soccer World Cup. It was time for Africa and it was going to happen. The focus of the world was going to be on the continent. It suddenly struck me that our new LED lighting technology had advanced far enough for us to light a small football pitch using solar powered batteries.

This would address a number of needs, including sustainability, and be just in time for the soccer World Cup. Our brand and technology might resonate across the world! As far as I knew, this would also be a world first. Never before had natural sunlight powered a game of football after dark in Africa. This was an exciting idea.

I first approached some of our managers with this. They nodded encouragingly, but were clearly too busy to spend any time on it. Therefore, I decided to run with the idea myself. Could it be done?

I approached a number of our technical people, who confirmed that we could. Then I needed funding to develop a prototype. I called on our chief technology officer who gave his support. A Moroccan colleague called Mohammed, starting drawing up plans and designs, and we worked out the details in an atmosphere of excitement.

We could light an area of 1000 square metres (or forty by twenty five metres) to a level about five times higher than normal street lighting. This would use the latest LED lighting at the time, along with solar panels and batteries. We continued to work on suppliers during the summer and autumn of 2009. Technically all this was in addition to my day job, but it started taking up more and more of my time.

In late June, I managed to squeeze in the Kilimanjaro climb with Roger. Larry was also there from our 'Save the Snow' trip, with a couple of friends.
A young, Dutch couple and a colleague called Marinelle made up the group. I recall we arrived at Nairobi airport on the morning that the news broke about Michael Jackson's death.

It was a strictly 'no sight-seeing' trip and we were on the hill within twenty-four hours of arrival. Our route was the Machame, which is, without doubt in my opinion, the most beautiful of those I had experienced.
We aimed to complete this in six days, instead of the seven, which I would now advise, and it proved far tougher than the Rongai.
My perception here may have been influenced by the fact that I was also very unfit. The only exercise I had done in the months before, had been my daily cycle ride to work and I had gained so much weight that I was now almost at a record three figures (in kilos).

For several days, we worked our way along the undulating flank of Kili – the side with the classic view – until we reached the camp below the Barranco wall. For the first time I had to use my hands to climb, and I enjoyed the prospect although of course it turned out to be a lot easier than it looked.
After that, it became a marathon of pain. We left the Barranco camp at 07.00 and for the next thirty-six hours, we were on the move for twenty-nine.
I had never experienced such an intensity of effort. We did not arrive at the Barafu hut at 4600 m until 19.00 after a hard twelve hours. We then had four-hour rest, including trying to eat before setting off for the summit about 23.30. I then disconcerted my

companions by being physically sick in the mess tent just before we set off.

We climbed through the night and it was bitterly cold. Above 5500 m, the wind was biting, chilling and going through my duvet jacket. I started to worry about frostbite.

None of us spoke. We suffered in worlds of our own, where the only dim thought, which flickered through our minds, was 'keep going.'

I had to dig as deep as I ever had, but simply could not contemplate stopping. Mental strength is indeed a key-asset in these circumstances. Finally, a few hours after dawn we stepped out on to the 5739 m summit at Stella Point.

The weather was perfect. Before us, lay the route to Uhuru peak, which was some forty minutes away up a gentle slope. We could see what looked like one hundred and fifty people queuing up along the route, with a long wait at the summit post, and I suddenly lost interest in going over to it.

Stella point was quiet and peaceful. We sat alone in the sun and relaxed looking into the summit crater. Our guide asked us what we wanted to do, and to his evident relief, we collectively decided not to bother.

I do not regret this decision, although it meant technically my fourth ascent of Kili was a silver medal.

We still had a long way to go that day. Our descent took us from 5739 m down to 3100 m at the Mweka hut. Again there was little talking. We rested at the Barafu camp for ninety mins and finally arrived, in a daze, at the lower camp around dusk at 18.30. It was low enough to start smelling my socks, which was not a good thing.

I felt as tired as I ever had been, by the effort involved, but at least Roger finally had his Kili summit-crater photo.

The following day we descended quickly to the park gates and headed out for the journey back to Nairobi. Some forty-eight hours later, I was behind my desk at work again. It had been an intense nine days. This time my tiredness lasted for weeks.

Team ID, including JR, James and Mark, along with Hugo and Nick, were in Saas Fee in July. They were keen that I join them, but I knew I did not have the strength or fitness. The lads climbed a number of for us new 4000 m peaks, including the Strahlhorn and the Nadelhorn and I stayed well informed of progress. However, I had already made my own choice that summer.

We spent our family holiday in Cornwall. Agata, Katie and I visited Terence and Joanne down at their flat in Cornwall and Terrence and I had a memorable day out, boating from Lostwithiel on the river Fowey down to Fowey itself, with our three young daughters, and being stuck in the middle of the estuary as the tide receded.

They loved it. We managed after a lot of effort, to avoid becoming newspaper headlines.

On returning to work, we then learned that our department was to be 'restructured' and that we would all be losing our jobs within six months. In the jargon used at the time, we were 'decentralizing' and our roles 'would be done' in future in Africa.

This was disappointing news. We would have either to find a new position within the company, or leave with an extraordinarily generous – from British eyes at least –and legally sanctioned, Dutch redundancy-package. Many of my more elderly colleagues were smiling, knowing early retirement beckoned.

I was determined to continue with my Africa work and was, by now firmly operating on a 'don't ask for permission' basis. This meant ignoring this hanging sword of Damocles and speeding things up.

That autumn we made good progress on the 'Africa-football-under-solar-lights' project. We designed a mobile solution, consisting of four floodlights on poles and powered by solar panels and batteries.

We found a contact with the Dutch Football Association, who linked us to a project in a Nairobi slum. This seemed a very good place to start. At the same time, we planned a second demonstration in South Africa near Johannesburg, where a number of very famous ex-Dutch soccer internationals, who happened to be touring, agreed to take part in a 'five a side' game against the local kids.

We planned a third demonstration with one of Africa's most influential footballers of all time. This would take place, along with a press conference, in the PSV stadium in Eindhoven. Our kick-off, as it were, was timed for November.

Around this time, I also gave a battlefield tour at Arnhem for the officers and NCOs from a battalion of the British army. Things went well and I was subsequently invited back later in the year, to be the main speaker/act at an annual British Army dinner. This was in Cyprus. The theme in the mess was the battle of Arnhem and I had a fascinating few days at the base. The Brigadier turned out to be a fellow graduate from my university and I accompanied a tour of the demilitarized zone.

On November 9 2009, in the Mathare slum in Nairobi, Kenya, we made a small piece of history by enabling, 'the world's first game of soccer played at night under solar powered lighting'. Within a week, the other events had also proved successful. We had proved the concept and there was a good deal of local excitement. Suddenly young people in the slum had the prospect of playing sport in the evening after dark.

The possibilities were endless for if we could use sunlight to power lights in this way, there was in fact nothing we could not light, anywhere. For a time I pondered the next steps and was suddenly struck by my second big idea of the year.

What if we organized 'an overland Cape to Cairo roadshow' in 2010, the World Cup year for Africa?

We could take the mobile solar lights along with us and play football/soccer in the evenings with the local kids, all the way across the continent. We could also display other relevant solutions. This would combine an epic adventure on the classic route across the continent, with clear-cut business objectives and a strong sustainable development story. Suddenly the spin-offs seemed incalculable.

From a business point of view, we could connect with distributors and partners along the way and host demonstrations and events. It would support our brand positioning and offer huge social media potential.

"Can you also say 'yes' to my next big idea?"

Amidst the ruins of our department, I quickly sketched out a plan and budget. Instinctively, I did not tell our middle management at this stage, fearing a knee jerk 'no' reaction as they wrestled with the dismantling of our team.

We would need to hire an overland-trekking company and I set about making enquiries. Then there was the big question of which route to take. It was soon clear that the only practical route would be down through East Africa.

We could start in Cairo and go via Kenya, Uganda, Rwanda, and Tanzania down through Malawi, Zimbabwe, and Botswana to South Africa.

I then calculated how long this would take and decided that it would be difficult to justify the time between Cairo and Nairobi – so decided we would fly this bit. Even so, it meant a minimum two-month journey. I wondered how people would view an absence of two months travelling through Africa on full pay!

Other elements of the plan began to fall into place. The equipment we needed would be sent ahead to Nairobi. The best timing for the trip would be mid-May to July and the media and communications plan was relatively straightforward.

My main aim was to demonstrate to people what was now possible with new technology, and the stories, which flowed from this were obvious.

I would need to contact our distributors and the Dutch embassies and consulates in our target countries. Insurance and risk assessment would be required, and I knew I would need a good team to travel with.

I also created a short promotional film, explaining our objectives and intended to inspire those whose consent I knew I would ultimately need.

With the basis of a plan and budget in place, I knew my biggest task would be to get permission from at least one senior executive. This needed careful consideration. It was logical to start with our management in Africa, who 'owned' this business region and I went there first. To my relief, they were positive.

More good news came in late November. I was interviewed for and offered a new job in our corporate headquarters in Amsterdam. I would be responsible for communication in Africa for our division, and my new boss Andre was very interested in the 'Cape to Cairo' proposals.

It was crucially a role, which would allow me to continue the work, and I would not need a plan B. This was probably just as well; as I have often heard that plan, B's are not my strong point.

That Christmas, Agata, Katie and I splashed out on a skiing holiday in Banff, Canada. My main memory now is being discharged from a hospital in Calgary, one hundred km from our hotel, with three broken ribs at 05.00 wearing only my underpants and a T-shirt and with -20C outside.

Surplus clothes, which their previous owners clearly did not need, and a taxi, were procured to save the day. This made for a costly and painful start to 2010.

If the pace of life and work had been fast in 2009, it became frenetic in those first months of the New Year. I remember a blur of meetings and long, long, days. I met several potential partners and decided to invest in a tour ambassador. We managed to secure Ruud Gullit, one of the Netherlands greatest soccer legends. Detailed plans evolved and I realized we were going somewhat over budget.

I had spent some time on selecting the team. Given the time away, it would be difficult to get direct company colleagues. We did a deal with a top soccer agency in Amsterdam to provide a couple of young lads to manage the football events and the clinics we planned. Rob, a financial director who was leaving the company and was keen to be involved, joined me. The overland travel company would provide a driver and guide. I also invited Jane from the 'Save the Snow' project knowing she had invaluable Africa experience and a never-ending supply of good humour.

Then for selected stages, others would join us for parts of the journey. An Egyptian colleague Mohammed would join for the first two weeks. In Rwanda, we would meet up with a Dutch journalist I knew, who would be 'embedded' with us for ten days until we reached Dar-Es-Salaam.

In Malawi my old boss Guido, who had been supportive throughout, would join us.

In February, a new colleague joined me on the project. Radhika came from India and worked for our Healthcare Division. She was strong, competent, enthusiastic and confident – just what the project needed. She would not travel overland but would meet us at selected sites for events, and would take a lot of the organizing burden from me.

Despite this, by late April, my stress levels were starting to rise and I decided to go to the UK for a few days with my parents and extended family to re-energize. We walked up Ingleborough in the Yorkshire Dales and I was very proud of young Katie who kept going through a few pain barriers, a real chip off the old block! This break really worked in putting some perspective back in life.

As things got closer, colleagues and managers became more involved. People really became enthusiastic about the adventure we were about to set out on. It was impressive to see my Company responding so positively to the idea of mixing adventure, risk-taking and business.

What had started out as a simple idea, driven by a passion for improving life, mixed with adventure, had turned into a huge and complicated undertaking. During the next few months we were going to travel from Cairo to Cape Town, demonstrating some really cool developments in terms of LED lighting and healthcare, which had the potential to transform life in Africa at a social and economic level.

Nor would we be alone, backed as we were by our ambassadors, partners, distributors and good colleagues both in Africa and in Amsterdam. We would be covering the classic route from North to South with more than eleven thousand km of road, visiting ten countries along the way and hosting twenty-three formal events. In addition, I was going to attempt to manage all this from a blackberry mobile phone!

I recorded in my blog just before we started out 'I don't expect this journey to be easy but it feels right at so many levels.'

Just before leaving for Cairo and the starting line, a colleague came over and congratulated me saying,

"This is going to be the highlight of your career".

I was tempted to reply with a smile "It could be the end of my career"

But I managed to stay positive.

As with most risk-taking ventures, there were a good many eyes watching us, and the pressure was on.

Above: The world's first game of football played at night under solar powered LED lighting. Nov 2009

Below: Giving the kids something new to do and see at night.

Above: The start of our Cape to Cairo roadshow road show in 2010. Shortly after this photo, the horse threw me off due to my weight!

Below: The inside of our overland vehicle for the journey.

3. Cape to Cairo - the first half   2010

Cairo was a great place to be; warm, friendly and full of life. Our hotel was on the Nile and the whole event had a regal feel to it. The launch went well: a series of media briefings, exhibitions and product demonstrations.

More than two hundred key people attended and our local Egyptian team did us proud. Afterwards we relaxed on the Nile and it was strange to think that, within 10 days or so, we would be visiting its source at Lake Victoria. Radhika and I also visited the Pyramids.

This was purely symbolic, as we wanted a photograph of ourselves at this iconic site. (The local authorities do not permit promotional activity with the Pyramids in the background). I recall one incident clearly.

On our way back, we visited a shop and were greeted in perfect English by the owner, whose party-piece was to call out to everyone who entered the name of a famous person that he thought they most closely resembled. In my case, he took one look and called out 'Winston Churchill!'

After this, we flew down to Nairobi. We arrived on Sunday evening 16 May 2010 and immediately experienced Nairobi's biggest issue: road traffic congestion. Just a warning to anyone planning anything here! It can take two hours to drive ten km.

Here I met up with our overland team, who were already waiting. They were Nev and Carol, our driver guide combination, lent to us by our overland trekking friends. Nev was a hard working Aussie, a farmer by trade who was spending a few years driving around the Middle east and Africa. He would do most of the driving.

Carol was British, and taking a few years off from working in the National Health Service. Both were in their early 30's, easy-going and very unfamiliar with the corporate world, which was about to descend upon them.

Jane and Rob joined us, along with the two Dutch lads called Netherlands' Nick and Frank. Our final companion for the first part was Mohammed, our friendly Egyptian colleague, who, although well versed in travelling around central Africa had never slept in a tent before. There was a good team click from the start.

I left the guys to finish the final preparations loading our overland vehicle with equipment, and went off for a few days to the corporate-world. After the usual round of media briefing, training, lobbying and customer briefings, I joined our own Africa management team for an internal planning meeting. That evening I had arranged a special game of football for them.

"Oh and by the way….this evening we're going to play football against the world soccer street champions!"

After work, we would visit Mathare - one of the largest slums in Nairobi - and play a game of five-a-side football against the local youth from the MYSA (Mathare Youth Sports Association). The game of course would take place under our solar-powered LED lighting, after dusk.

I then dropped my bombshell. 'MYSA are the reigning street soccer world champions'. The faces on my middle-aged colleagues were worth it! In the end, we managed to lose gracefully and without shame.

With this out of the way, we were able to start on our journey. Our first stop was to be in Iten, the high altitude training area for Kenyan Olympic athletes. Locally born Dutch athlete, world and Olympic champion, Lornah Kiplegat and her Dutch husband Pieter, had invited us to visit them at their training base and play a game of football.

I noted with interest that the roads in this part of Kenya had improved significantly in the past four years since I had been there last and there seemed to be good internet coverage.

We arrived about 16:30 and just had time to set up the lights on an adjacent field, before the daylight started to fade. Lornah and Pieter were great hosts, as well as inspirational people, and they had, as we discovered, made many good arrangements.

There were many dignitaries present including heads of schools, the Kenyan army and journalists of the leading Kenyan newspapers and TV.

We asked the local district commissioner to switch on the lights - a moment of minor tension on our side! However, everything worked perfectly. An estimated two thousand local people had come to see what was happening.

There were games with the local kids, a soccer clinic from Dutch Nick and Frank and, in the end lots of people got involved. It was a real party atmosphere. Meanwhile I was busy giving media interviews and briefings. I lost count in the end but it was at least six interviews for TV. Radhika and our healthcare team were also present and gave their own interviews too.

At the end of the evening, we were invited to stay another day, something we decided we could fit into our schedule.

The following morning we visited the regional school awards. Some twelve hundred-school children, in colourful school uniforms, were present, sitting patiently in the grass besides the school. It was a scorching hot day and Lornah, who was of course a local celebrity, said a few words and then invited me to present our solar-powered reading light. It was the largest gathering I had ever addressed.

That evening we sat together, watching Kenyan TV news reporting on our own event the previous evening. We were all over the various channels and it felt strange to watch oneself talking on air.

The next day we headed out for Uganda. By now, we were ready for a break and this would involve a couple of days camping at Jinja on the river Nile.

We would be recharging our batteries both literally and metaphorically by going white-water rafting downstream from the source of the river. Our team spirit was by now really starting to develop and it was becoming obvious how much 'Africa experience' we had amongst us. This gave me a huge confidence boost.

Our day out on the river was sensational; a real fun, exciting, adventure, with team singing and a few capsizes over the huge rapids. This was not white-water rafting for the faint hearted. Some of the sheer drops were twenty foot or so.

Near the start and left by the British was a huge statue of John Speke, the Victorian explorer who had 'found Lake Victoria'. Being British I had been brought up with epic tales of how the mid-19th century explorers such as Livingstone, Burton, Speke, Baker and Stanley 'discovered the Central African lakes and hence the source of the Nile'.

How ridiculous this suggestion actually was had become clear to me a few years before, when I saw Dutch maps of Africa from the 17th and 18th centuries, long before Livingstone et al, clearly showing lakes already marked.

In addition, this is not even to mention the fact that Africans knew these places since the dawn of time. We should always be prepared to question and challenge!

Our few days of rest were soon over and it was back to the corporate experience. It was only a short distance to Kampala and its hills and for the record, we arrived there on May 24 2010. Meetings followed with our tour partners from the 'Right to Play Foundation', our distributors and local NGOs.

In between this, we were doing laundry, catching up on emails and repairing our truck's gearbox and a dozen other jobs. The people were friendly and inquisitive.

Some 88 percent of the Ugandan population, it was estimated lived without electricity and we had impression that we could have sold a truckload of solar-powered lights on the nearest corner, based on the reaction of the hotel staff.

Our Guest of Honour for the next day's event was the Ugandan Minister of State for Energy. In addition, we had about 50 other key stakeholders attend our Healthcare/Lighting briefing.

The minister was very positive and kicked off the first game of football ever played in Uganda under solar-powered floodlighting.

This was a claim we made in each country we visited and many journalists were there to capture the moment.

Kampala confirmed for me how well our overland team fitted together. They were superb: Frank, 'Netherlands Nick', Jane, Carol, Nev, Rob and Mohammed were the right people for the job.

Just a word on Uganda: after its difficult recent history, the country appeared to be moving forward. Significant quantities of oil had been found; the people were very friendly and the countryside was stunning.

Later on when people asked, me, which was the most attractive country I had travelled through, my answer, was always unhesitatingly 'Uganda'. Moreover, there was to be one more bonus from a climbing point of view. Sometime soon on our drive south, we would have an opportunity to glimpse the Mountains of the Moon.

I remembered how we had briefly considered these hills for an expedition back in 1999. 'Too wet' had been the general verdict at the time and we had chosen for the Andes instead.

We left Kampala very early to avoid traffic, and breakfasted on the equator a few hours later. Joel, a journalist from the best-selling Dutch newspaper 'De Telegraaf', based in South Africa, had now joined us. He was a very astute observer of African life. I knew Joel from a trip we had done together to Northern Ghana a few years before, and he would now be travelling with us until Dar es Salaam, recording his experiences and we hoped providing a positive view on our efforts. He was friendly, open and likeable, with a great sense of humour.

We travelled to within thirty minutes of the Rwandan border before putting up our tents for the night. We also needed time to recharge our batteries before the upcoming Kigali event!

That evening we gained another insight into the mainly youthful world of overland trekking.

Rather like ships briefly meeting at sea, a fellow group of travelers from Nev and Carol's company joined us in the campsite for the evening. They had been travelling up from Rwanda and were heading for Cairo.

The whole thing developed into a mass party, which went on into the early hours.

It was therefore with sore heads that we crossed the border into Rwanda the next morning.

I had been looking forward to seeing Rwanda more than any other place we were set to visit. To our minds, it represented hope for the future, after rising from the ashes of a most horrendous genocide, which had taken place only sixteen years earlier.

The world had been wrong-footed at the time and had delayed its own response for far too long.

Since then it had been changing in several important ways. Firstly, tribal boundaries were being broken down. The young people we met all said they were Rwandans, rather than Tutsis or Hutus. The second thing was that the country was switching from speaking French to speaking English. This was leading to a cultural split in the generations.

As we approached the capital Kigali, the countryside became steep and hilly and was dotted with tea plantations. It was also remarkably clean due, as we were to find out, to the new policy of having all citizens spend one Sunday morning a month cleaning up and working on public projects. As chance would have it, one such Sunday would be the day we were due to leave.

In Kigali, I recall we did all the corporate events we had planned. The Dutch consulate gave us great support. Incidentally, we had contacted the Dutch consulates for all the countries we were visiting well in advance, and found a mixed reception, with some going out of their way to help, whilst others virtually ignored us.

However, I have two memories that really stand out from this visit. One occurred in my four star hotel room, in the city centre. I say 'my room' but as I was to discover I was not alone in that assumption. I was sitting on the edge of my bed watching the BBC news on the TV, when I noticed out of the corner of my eye a smallish snake coming towards me.

It seemed very hostile and suddenly reared up. Instinctively I threw a cushion at it and it slithered away behind a cupboard. I pondered what to do and then rang the reception to report I had a snake in my room.

They said they would send someone and as I was not going to chase it behind the cupboard I sat down and resumed my TV watching. No sooner had I done so and I saw it again coming at me in an even more aggressive manner.

This time I decided to take action. Grabbing the rather large, tall, plastic waste bin, which happened to be in the room I scooped up the snake into it. It was satisfying to watch it try and fail to climb out.

As this seemed to be out of the ordinary I took a photo of the snake in the bin and waited.

Some ten minutes later, there was a knock on the door and in came a hotel worker, decked out in a full body suit and gloves as if he was responding to a nuclear accident. He rushed in and asked in French where the snake was.

I pointed to the waste paper bin and he visibly jumped at the site of it. I then asked him what it was and all he would say was 'tres dangereux....tres dangereux'. He very carefully placed the bin into a huge sack and disappeared.

The photo would later identify a small black mamba – one of the most dangerous snakes in Africa and one of the few that is said to attack without you upsetting it. It had probably come into my room I noted, via a tree branch overhanging my balcony.

The hotel said nothing more about it, although their response suggested they were used to such intrusions and I decided not to make an issue of it.

I did carefully scan the room for its parents, but after finding, nothing decided to stay put for the night. Had I known then that close to two hundred thousand people, worldwide, die of snakebites each year I would not have been so relaxed.

Therefore, he scooped the snake into the waste paper bin!

That evening we had a curry with our distributor, whose name was Salim. He had survived the 1994 genocide and during our meal, he talked about it. "The first thing you should know" he said "was that that it was planned. They came round armed with machetes and with lists of names. I was not on their list and so they let me go" Salim then described some of the horrors he had witnessed, although I suspect he also held a lot back from us. For sheer sadism, these stories rivaled those I had read about in the Nazi holocaust and it seemed difficult to imagine in the well-ordered city of today, that this had happened only sixteen years before.

Fortunately, for Salim he had finally managed to escape to Uganda with his family. This had only been a small part of our conversation that evening but it remained the dominant impression.

I do not think any of us who were there will forget it. This together with my snake experience meant sleep was difficult to come by that night. .

We left Kigali early on a Sunday morning and witnessed the reality of the whole country being up and on the move, working hard on cleaning and maintaining things. At times, we saw hundreds of people marching along the side of the road with equipment in their hands, to a work site; the atmosphere seemed calm and orderly.

On the truck there had been a small change of cast with 'Netherlands' Nick and Frank returning home, and being replaced by their colleagues Jasper and Bas, also Dutch by the way, who would do the same role of football-coaching for the rest of the journey.

Mohammed also left for home, but the rest of us now faced a massive journey. I now recalled my 19th century Victorian history lessons again.

We were now going to cross Tanzania from Central Africa to the coast at Dar es Salaam. This was roughly the same route taken by Burton and Speke in 1856-58. They had spent six months travelling the distance we now had to cross in a few days.

We would also be experiencing our first bush camps. The countryside was undulating and endless, and we travelled for twelve hours on the first day, stopping only briefly for lunch. The roads were uniformly bad, with Nev claiming they were the worst he had ever experienced.

Our overland vehicle received a terrific shaking all day long, and I started to worry about our LED floodlights. Could they survive such a hammering?

That evening we stopped at dusk by the side of the road and pitched our tents. We had just finished dinner, when a local police vehicle approached us and stopped. Out jumped three armed men and came towards us. Carol, who knew well what was coming, told us she would manage this.

The police said we could not stay where we were, as it was 'too dangerous' and they could not 'guarantee our safety'. Therefore, we would have to strip the camp and drive 30 miles in the dark, to their compound at a nearby town.

Carol firmly declined the offer politely claiming we could not move. After a while, it became a standoff with both sides just repeating their positions. Slowly we then entered negotiations. Yes we could stay where we were, but we would need protecting became the theme.

In addition, this would cost money of course. It was settled that three armed police officers would camp with us and patrol our campsite all night and be provided with dinner for an agreed sum. Our Tanzanian 'friends' whooped with joy as the deal was struck.

One of my most abiding memories of the trip is of Carol, standing up un-flinchingly to these armed men and negotiating us out of trouble. It was a magnificent spectacle. Our self-appointed guards then put on a big show of patrolling 'the perimeter' of our camp.

We slept early, well and left before dawn. Our guards by now were all asleep in an old tent we had decided to 'donate' too, so we never did get to say goodbye. 'They don't get paid for months in these parts' was Carol's sympathetic comment.

The second day was if anything, even longer than the first. Hour after hour of bumpy, bone shaking driving, punctuated only by occasional switches of driver and lunch. I do remember seeing, for the first time, the Chinese involvement in East Africa.

A new tarmac road was being built and the men working on it were all Chinese. The stories appeared to be true. They had brought their own labour with them from home.

Well after dark, we arrived at the 'snake-pit camp' near Arusha. It had a bar called Ma and Pa and we quickly settled down to some beers. The campsite was full of fellow overlanders from all parts of the world and soon the stories starting flowing.

"Whew.....I'm glad we had these guys looking after us!"

Several Europeans had just died of cerebral malaria in the very campsite we were staying at. This was concerning, as we were heading for the mosquito-infested coast of East Africa. Most of us had stopped taking our anti-malaria drugs due to the side effects.

The next morning my first task was to check our LED floodlights. To my relief and actual amazement, they had all survived the pounding they had received. I could not imagine that traditional lights would have managed this.

After a rest day in Arusha, we headed for Dar es Salaam. For several hours, we drove in the shadow of the Kilimanjaro. It was

71

the first time in my life I could see it looming up knowing I would not be climbing it. We had initially considered taking a week off to do so but had decided against it as being too long to justify.

It had been a heavy rain season that spring and Tanzania was looking particularly green. We camped next to the road half way to 'Dar' and cooked *'bangers and mash'* by the side of the truck. Our destination that day was a local community, some forty km outside of Dar es Salaam. We had been invited whilst already travelling.

This was done by a fellow Brit called Richard, who was the CEO of a bio-fuels start-up, who was keen to demonstrate that our LED floodlights could also be run, using a bio-fuels generator. The community was present along with the local MP and a hundred other key stakeholders, TV-media and our team. It promised to be an interesting night!

I think that none of our group who was there will ever forget the next few hours. More than a thousand people came to see the event, the highlight of which turned out to be a 'grudge match' between two local villages.

It was, again, we claimed, the first ever football tournament in Tanzania played under solar-powered LED lighting.

As the evening progressed, the people watching became more and more excited. There was communal singing, dancing, regular pitch invasions and celebrations when goals were scored. It was a joyous, life-enhancing, nerve-racking experience, which is difficult to describe.

Our own team was again superb and I was very conscious how little control we had over things. Fortunately, the local team hosting won the game, which probably prevented a riot. It was a remarkable demonstration of how much emotion can be created by combining light and football.

The next day was to be Joel's last day with us and we dropped him off at Dar es Salaam airport. He had been a great companion these past ten days and he subsequently wrote a full page and very positive piece for his newspaper. I was particularly glad that he had witnessed the previous evening.

The next few days were full of corporate activities. Radhika was there too, and so were the TV cameras. A team also joined us from our partners from the Right-To-Play Foundation. Deborah, a Dutch judo star and Olympics World Championship medalist, joined us and was a brilliant ambassador. She spoke to the press and took part in the football games with great enthusiasm. The atmosphere was relaxed and important discussions were ongoing.

We also witnessed at first hand the excellent work this foundation does.

We were invited to visit a school play day at a school in 'Dar' with about four hundred children, aged about eight to twelve. They were being instructed on key social issues such as malaria, HIV/Aids and conflict resolution, using games and role-play. I remember addressing a group of about twenty kids with a couple of teachers and asking who had already had malaria. Almost every hand went up.

From our hotel rooms we could see the Indian Ocean just a few hundred metres away, lapping the local beaches. We would not see the sea again until Durban in South Africa!

So far so good! We were heading for Malawi and our next big event in Lilongwe.

The core of the team remained for the second half of our journey. Carol and Nev, Jane, Rob, Jasper, Bas and I as we set off for what would be a long drive south.

Above: The main aim of the road show was to display what solar powered LED lighting could do for rural communities.

Below: Egypt was the starting point for our corporate events

Above – we practiced what we preached – loading batteries in Uganda.

Below: White water rafting at the source of the Nile in Uganda.

Above: Tanzania -the two local villages played under the lights.

Below: Our corporate event in Dar Es Salaam.

Above: Uganda – One of about 20 TV interviews I did on the way.

Below: Uganda – meeting the then Minister of Energy who kicked off the game.

4. Cape to Cairo - the second half and extra time. 2010

It is a well-known fact to Africa travelers, that the Mercator lines grossly distort the size of the continent on our world maps and that its real size is not represented.

The reality of this was literally driven home to us during the next few days, as we spent long, long, days in the truck and then checked each evening to find we had only covered about a centimeter on our map.

The pace was ideal though, and the sights and sounds of southern Tanzania and Northern Malawi drifted past at a slow and steady pace.

We had by now long settled into a daily routine of lunch stops by the side of the road and nights spent in tents or lodges – which in general we preferred, although we had to live with geckos, spiders and the like crawling along the walls of our rooms, which were always open to the elements somewhere.

In normal circumstances, this would have been off-putting, but now I merely shrugged my shoulders and slept soundly.

Our truck had been the center of our lives for almost a month now, and had become cozily familiar.

Carol, we had discovered, was a remarkable young woman. She was totally at ease in Africa and controlled all our logistics.

Except for our own customer events, we followed her orders.

She briefed us regularly on what we were going to do and where each day, and during stops she had us all doing the necessary chores. It was superb, natural leadership.

Hygiene was a key factor, with mandatory washing of hands and cleaning of all food surfaces a major feature.

I can only say that after almost a month, none of our party had been ill yet, despite the fact that most of us had long since stopped taking our malaria pills.

Our food was local and bought along the way and our friendly Aussie Nev, who never used a map, but seemed to be working on some internal compass, did most of the driving or maybe it was the sun. In a sense, it did not matter as long as we headed south. Whilst driving we could read, talk, discuss, listen to music on the iPod speakers and work on laptops or Blackberries and generally enjoy the luxury of being able to really think about things and new ideas. In addition, we had plenty of new insights each day to consider.

All this was facilitated by moving in an open top vehicle through wonderfully inspiring landscapes and passing warm friendly people everywhere. A smile and a wave is a universal human interaction. It was noticeable how young Africa is, as old people were a rarity. The young are naturally optimistic and this was infectious. It made us feel that anything was possible and we mulled over new ideas on a daily basis.

After three such days, we arrived at a campsite on the shores of Lake Malawi for a couple of rest days. Here in the bar we got talking. We were always talking to lots of people we met about life and consequently had been gaining many insights.

One of these was that the local women's netball teams in the immediate area were very good and the National Malawi team was in the world top ten. On hearing about our lights, it was decided with the locals over some beers that we would organize an impromptu tournament.

Therefore, we made history again by playing the first ever game of netball at night, under solar powered lights. It was our 'Cape to Cairo' team against the young women in question.

It soon became obvious they were indeed very good for, despite being only about half our size and age, they ran rings around us and beat us easily. The passion and excitement on the faces was memorable.

The second 'first' we were able to claim, was the first-ever game of beach volleyball under solar powered lights. This was our attempt to ingratiate ourselves with our fellow travelers, who were also staying in the campsite. Being closer to the bar, this was a more alcoholic occasion but no less fun for that.

One other memory remains. I remember seeing dark clouds, looking like waterspouts across Lake Malawi, which seemed strange, set against the sunny blue sky in general. I asked what these were and was told they were giant swarms of lake flies, which are a very common site over the northern part of the lakeshore. Apparently, the fly larvae live on the lake bottom, where they feed, after which they float to the surface and hatch all at once causing the giant swarms of millions. Essentially, they are flying food as the swarms attract fish and many species of birds that feed off them.

I asked what happened if they came ashore and learned that people caught them in nets and baskets and squashed them together to create a local delicacy, which is fried and is rich in protein.

I cannot say we knowingly ate any of these during our stay but it would have been fun to try some.

No doubt, someone can explain why they should have evolved in this way but it seems an odd sort of life – a few hours of flying around with a million competitors, just to serve as fish food or end up in a protein burger for the locals.

Football was everywhere and during our customer event in Lilongwe a couple of days later, the soccer World Cup kicked off in South Africa. We were still several thousand kilometers from Johannesburg, but the local support was for the hosts and people were proclaiming their loyalties loudly and passionately in all the bars and hotels and in the streets.

Although we had timed our event to finish in time for the

opening game, it was in hindsight a miracle that we still got about sixty people to come to our customer event in a good Lilongwe hotel, including business contacts, banks, NGOs contractors, and end users. Top media, TV and print were also present.

More insights into Malawi, sales leads and ideas were generated! However, football dominated even in our business conversations and it became clear what the universal language in Africa really is.

I found Malawi a beautiful country with very friendly people and was sad when we had to leave. By now, we had been reinforced by the enthusiasm and experience of my ex-boss Guido. A tall Dutchman, with a great sense of vitality and humour, he would provide a real boost to our energy levels. Proof of this was almost immediate, as on leaving Lilongwe, we suffered our one and only truck breakdown of the entire trip, something that was immediately blamed on Guido. He laughed this off in masterly fashion.

We crossed the border into Zambia and bush camped that night near a quarry. For once I was kept awake for a long time by the noises of animals, scratching around outside. Lying in my sleeping bag in the middle of the night, senses alert, I recorded the following blog on my blackberry

'The Art of Corporate Bush-camping, June 15, 2010

Imagine that you are in a good quality hotel, armed with your laptop and presentations, and suited with your freshly ironed shirt and tie. You are talking to a government minister or a key NGO representative and demonstrating why LED lighting offers simple life- enhancing solutions for local issues. You have access to hot water, showers, electric light, a restaurant and bar. You are modern 'corporate man/woman' in a 'normal' environment.

Now imagine less than 24 hours later, that you are 500 kms away in the middle of nowhere. You are going to bush-camp (camp randomly) somewhere by the side of a dusty road and suddenly none of your Power Point presentational skills are remotely relevant. Africa is renowned for its hostile nature in these circumstances.

Consider where to best pitch your tent to avoid wild animals, insects – you have seen many 'new to you' species of things you don't want to share your sleeping bag with. Consider the need to avoid upsetting local people or being run over in the dark by a truck, the lights of which have failed, and the driver thinks your side turning might be the road.

Then you also need to get a fire going, so you can cook your food, before it goes dark at 1800. There is of course no electric light, running water, showers, or washing, other than brushing your teeth. You need to transform yourself into 'bush camp man/woman' and fast.

Then, once the fire gets going, so does the conversation and for a while you are hypnotized by an ancient ritual. You will practice what you preach after dark by using a solar-powered LED light but despite everything, you will still be in your tent by 0800, as it will be cold. In addition, the night is long. You cannot possibly sleep for all of it and you will hear every sound outside your tent. Moreover, there are many noises…

Somewhere during all of this, your mind will turn to the fact that within a couple of days, at most, of your current situation, you will be in another hotel in a different country, with new stakeholders and back in 'corporate men/women' mode. You will need a newly ironed shirt and a few dozen other key details

sorting out. Then, as you are considering all this, you will hear
something new outside your tent!

Flexibility of mind is simply enforced here. Welcome to the
fascinating, inspiring and challenging world of the 'Africa
Roadshow!'

Bush camping means hearing every sound outside your tent –
and misinterpreting it!

Our three days in Zambia are now just a blur of memories. The
customer event in Lusaka, with the Government Minister, who
did the kick-off at our football game (the first ever under solar
lights in Zambia …..) and the applause he received for his very
neat, ball-juggling abilities.
Guido being asked by the Minister, to come back and develop a
major infrastructure project and the live radio interviews I did
right after the news, which went out locally.
We also said goodbye to our trusted companions Bas and Jasper,

who were returning to the Netherlands, after doing a great job. For the last part of the journey, we would be down to six.

Other impressions included the friendly, smiling and welcoming faces of people around us, and very noticeably the change in the colour of the countryside from green to dusty brown.

I remember too, crossing the Zambesi river, which was very wide and blue and imagined David Livingstone, heading up it towards the Victoria Falls just over a hundred years before me or just forty years before my grandmother was born.

We soon reached the border crossing into Zimbabwe, where I noted a UK citizen paid big bucks for a visa whilst for the Dutch they were virtually free. Apart from this, it was actually a very efficient process. The buildings clearly dated from the colonial era and there were monkeys swarming all over the security fences.

We were all looking forward to visiting Zimbabwe and seeing how much of the media image of a country in disastrous ruin was true.

Our first impressions were that things seemed little different from the other countries we had just passed through. The main road seemed fine and we had no problem driving down to Harare, where we stopped at the city youth hostel.

Here we chose to camp in the grounds so as to, we pompously told ourselves, save corporate money. Our fellow overnighters were a mixture of young international travelers mixed with a few locals.

We were due to stay for a couple of days, as our truck would be going through a complete overhaul as our overland trekking team had a centre in Harare. We filled this time by meetings with our distributor, market research and with an unplanned and unexpected meeting with a close business associate of President Mugabe, which took place in a new supermarket, which had just been opened. We noted the streetlights were using incandescent lightbulbs.

By now, we had also noticed some of the issues. The country was living 'unofficially' on US dollars and you could even get these from the ATMs, as the local currency was effectively worthless. In fact, street traders were selling old Zimbabwean dollar notes, showing numbers from ten million to fifty million Zimbabwean dollars, as souvenirs for far more than their real value. It was clear too that sanctions and a lack of investment were having a significant impact and it was obvious why the Chinese were being courted.

"So I give you 10 US dollars – and you give me 100,000,000 Zimbabwean dollars? Sounds like a deal!"

Politically we were more aware of the story. Officially, at the time there was a power-sharing arrangement between the Prime Minister and the President, who otherwise stood opposed to each other. I heard a story one evening told by a young Zimbabwean about the recent soccer game, which he himself had witnessed. 'When the Prime Minister entered the stadium the whole crowd stood up and cheered' he said 'and when the President came in a few minutes later there was no reaction at all.'

However, that evening on the TV news the pictures had shown it the other way round with the President being cheered. "This is what happens here" he said.

The young Zimbabwean did not seem bitter, just resigned.

World Cup fever had also struck the country and the National Team had just played a friendly warm-up match against Brazil. We also spoke to a few white Zimbabwean families who had remained and seemed to be living active and outdoor lives. They confirmed there were less than ten thousand white people left and very few farmers.

Jane had already told us how people could not move their life savings out of Zimbabwe and she herself had attended a 'blow it all in style' party because of this.

Everywhere we went, we talked to the local people, learned about their lives and about how they viewed the need for lighting. I remember asking one local lad what light in the evening meant and he simply answered, "Everybody needs light and without it things cannot work". Imagine the economic boost to Africa if more than five hundred million people could extend their day by just a few hours.

That weekend we drove across Zimbabwe and stayed at a lodge near Bulawayo. It was now that the stunning beauty of the country became apparent, with green countryside and rolling hills.

The lodge offered a number of wildlife opportunities beyond the standard safari. Early in the morning, Guido and I went 'walking with lions.' These were being prepared for a return to the bush and we were provided with sticks and strict instructions on how to behave. This, along with a general lack of common sense, allowed us to both approach a large lion lying in the grass, from behind and stroke it.

On our way to Victoria Falls, we also spent a short night in Bulawayo with friends of Nev, where we camped in the gardens of a huge colonial-era house. It was run-down and seemed very out of place with its surroundings but our hosts were extremely friendly and welcoming. They talked about their lives and thoughts. Life in Zimbabwe today is challenging.

Victoria Falls itself was more difficult to describe. Words like 'awesome', 'stunning' and 'fantastic' somehow seem inadequate. It was without doubt the most impressive geographical site I had seen in Africa, if not the world. It is a place where the elephant (the spirit of Africa) just walks through the streets whilst monkeys were everywhere!

We paid out of our own pockets for a short helicopter ride over the falls, which was worth every US dollar. We experienced the enormous spray of the water as we walked around the rim; watched the bungie jumping from the bridge, and pondered the old-style statue to Dr. David Livingstone.

That night, an elephant walked right into and through our camp. I still have a blurry photo taken of this interesting event.

My other memory is how we had surprisingly good connectivity near the falls and how quite a few of us spent a day working and answering emails in the same way as we might have done sitting in our offices or at home. It gives a new twist to the idea of the working holiday!

We now faced a couple of long days in the truck before our next major event in Gaborone, Botswana.

Our introduction to the country was brutal. We had just settled down after crossing the border, when a car with a trailer raced past us at speed and disappeared off into the distance.

Nobody thought anything of it until Nev suddenly hit the brakes a few minutes later. Looking ahead, we could see a dead, baby elephant lying in the road. A few hundred yards beyond was the upturned car, which had recently passed us. The trailer and its contents were all across the road. We pulled up slowly. A father and three teenage children were huddled together by the side of the car in shock. The mother still lay in the car and Carol soon confirmed she was dead. They were Italians, soccer fans for the World Cup on their way back to South Africa.

Whilst this human tragedy was evolving, I was acutely aware an animal tragedy was taking place a few hundred yards away. A large herd of elephants had been crossing the road and the mother elephant was walking around and sniffing her dead baby, seemingly confused as if willing the calf to get up and start walking again.

Large bull elephants were also watching nearby. The thought flashed through my mind they might want revenge.

We quickly considered our options. There was no mobile coverage where we were, and we did not have a satellite link. The nearest medical facilities were more than an hour's drive away and the Italian family made it clear they did not want to leave the scene.

As none of them seemed physically injured, we decided to head on quickly to the nearest town and hospital to get help.

We offered them blankets but they refused and said they would await the official rescue services. By now, other drivers had arrived too.

It was still hard to imagine what had happened. It was daylight; full sunlight even. The road was good and cleared for about fifty metres on either side. Clearly, they must have seen the elephants.

I suspect the driver had kept driving at speed and had swerved around a larger elephant and had missed seeing the small baby elephant. The car had then hit it a lethal blow.

Incidentally, the term baby elephant makes it sound small, but as it lay there in the middle of the road, it was the size of several very large cows.

Nev pushed the revs as we sped off down the long, straight tarmac road; the only route to the nearest town.

We caught sight of new herds of elephants all the time and had been going for thirty minutes or so when we saw an ambulance and police cars heading up the road in the opposite direction, sirens ablaze. Clearly, someone had used a satellite phone.

That night we bush camped for the last time. Over our campfire, Carol told us that under the law the Italian family would probably be charged with the death of the elephant, which was protected by law, and would likely be sent the bill for the cost. It was like one of those moments when someone you know, who is not close family or friend, has suddenly died and you briefly stop your busy, hectic life and reflect on what is really important.

As a result of this reflection, most of us chose to sleep in the truck that night. In fact, only Carol slept out in her tent. She awoke refreshed – we did not. I had kept the others awake by snoring and they had kept me awake by kicking.

The next day, we arrived in the capital city Gaborone. On the way in, it was clear from the people, roads and infrastructure that Botswana was noticeably wealthier than its northern neighbours.

This however obscured a tragic secret. Aids was devastating the country, with an estimated one third of the young people under thirty suffering from the disease. In 2010, the average life expectancy was estimated at just thirty-eight. US aid was helping address the problem.

In addition to the World Cup – the newspapers were also full of stories about energy shortages. We aimed our corporate event at this. Our friends at the 'Right to Play Foundation' arranged for the under-twenty National Football Team to play under our solar lights.

As I watched, I began to realize how tired we all were. It was as if our energy had drained away and it was almost with a sense of relief that we packed away our roadshow items into the truck.

Our next step was to cross into South Africa and stop temporarily in Johannesburg. By now, we were back in the developed world and it all reminded me of the US.

Because the soccer World Cup was now on and we were not a FIFA sponsor we had decided not to conduct, any soccer related marketing activities in South Africa during this period. In football terms, our roadshow would be having a short break after 90 minutes, before moving into extra time.

For the record, we arrived in Johannesburg on June 28, 2010. We met Jan, from our South African team and had a final dinner together. Nev and Carol were heading on down to Cape Town for a short rest there, before picking up a new group, whom they would take all the way back up to Cairo.

The rest of us were flying home. I alone of the group would return to continue on the final leg.

Together we had travelled about nine thousand km through ten countries; had held eleven major and five minor events. We had talked to hundreds of people ranging from Government ministers, and officials, ambassadors, NGOs, business people and to the people living with, or without electricity, in all parts of the countries we have visited. The business opportunities seemed obvious and I felt confident that we had delivered a strong corporate statement.

The following two weeks I spent at home including a weekend visit to friends in the UK and my parents 50th wedding anniversary, felt surreal. The change was sudden and highlighted the differences between the Netherlands and the places we had visited.

I returned to Johannesburg on July 15. It was very quiet at Schiphol as I left. The Dutch had just lost the World Cup final to Spain, the third time in the past two generations and enough to give anyone Dutch a real hangover.

The story of the next two weeks can be briefly told.

I was accompanied by Anthony, a good colleague, and Mark, my Oasis contact who would also be our driver. The three of us clicked well and we became the three musketeers.

In Johannesburg, we organized an inter-company football-BBQ for the staff; held a corporate event and then headed off on a small, six hundred km hop towards Durban. It had been cold in Johannesburg, -2C had been recorded whilst we were there, but Durban was considerably warmer with the waves of the Indian Ocean lapping at lovely sandy beaches.

Here I came down with toothache and had a most instructive talk with a local Indian dentist who explained to me more about my teeth in twenty minutes than I had heard in the rest of my life put together until then. He also spent the next twenty minutes, digging one of my rear molars out, after it had splintered in situ. Staggering back to our event on anti-biotics, I then delivered a corporate speech and presentation to our stakeholders and somehow kept my end up.

The venue probably helped as it overlooked the sea and came complete with a golf course and palm trees. We had a very good turnout of local customers and demonstrated our outdoor solar-story on the lawn outside the country club.

We followed with the classic three-day seventeen hundred km drive along the coastal route of the East and West Cape to our final destination at Cape Town. At night, we stayed in Bed and Breakfast type accommodation and my only regret was not being able to drink a beer, due to the anti-biotics.

Cape Town proved a fitting finale for the Roadshow.

We arrived at our hotel and met two more colleagues - Garrett our senior executive, who had been on the 'Save the Snow' trip and Jan from the local team, who would support the final act.

We completed the corporate routine and then teamed up with the 'Stars in their Eyes' Foundation to provide a solar-powered soccer-lighting event for the local community of Piketburg, west of Cape Town.

The passion, excitement and enthusiasm displayed by the local kids proved a good reminder of why we had undertaken the roadshow in the first place.

As Radhika and I flew home from Cape Town, I reflected that in the ten weeks since we had started in Cairo, we had conducted twenty-one events in ten countries, and driven eleven thousand five hundred km.

I had given twenty TV interviews and we had generated hundreds of articles, along with significant social media outreach. Local feedback had been very positive, indeed passionate. We had talked to people at all levels of society, presidents and government ministers, NGOs and many other key influencers, but also the people living in the rural communities and city slums of this most remarkable continent.

It is impossible in these two chapters to describe anything but a small snapshot of all those impressions and insights. It had been simply the most fascinating journey of my life.

The 'Cape to Cairo' roadshow had been an immense undertaking. It had demonstrated that adventure, sport, and risk-taking can be combined effectively with corporate objectives. We had created sales leads, conducted research, supported distributors, generated an enormous amount of publicity and inspired many people within and without our company.

It was made possible by a great team, hard work, passion and enthusiasm. Most of the people with me had not been on salaries and had volunteered, because they believed in what we were trying to achieve.
It started as just an idea but we had found the people who could say 'yes'. Therefore, it happened.
By now mentally jaded I was looking forward to recovering by walking the hundred mile South Downs Way in the UK with Agata, James, Zoe Joanne and Terrence. My final thought on the trip was to look for some perspective.
One-day important areas of Africa will be lit at night using a network of solar-powered grids. This will enable social and economic development and be normal.
One day too Africa will provide the soccer world champions!
Back in 2010, we were one of the first to start demonstrating and talking about this.

Above: The team leaving Dar es Salaam. L-R Bas, Rob, Jane, Carol, Nev, Jasper and author.

Below: Zambia and the Dutch Ambassador kicked off the game

Above: Malawi - A memorable night playing netball against the local women's teams – we were thrashed.

Below: Our overland vehicle at a bush camp

Above: Zimbabwe stroking a lion – we had strict instructions on what to do. The lion had just had breakfast and was about to be released into the wild again.

Below: Vic falls from a helicopter. We paid for this ourselves!

Above: Radhika and I on Robben island at the end of the road show.

Below: A final and thoughtful bush camp in Botswana, the day of the accident.

5. Africa comes to Zermatt. 2011

I returned from Cape Town in late July 2010, uncertain of what kind of reception I was going to get from some of our management at the time. My main concern was that I had spent some 250,000 euro, which we did not have in our budget. The sack might be just as likely as plaudits. I would have to wait and possibly ask for forgiveness.

Reactions from my direct managers and colleagues though were almost universally positive. People were fascinated by our stories and by what we had shown could be done.

Corporate culture in general, at this time, was full of exhortations to think and act differently; to 'break the mould' of traditional thinking and our road, show was accepted as part of this.

It was as if we had broken through some invisible barrier, into new territory where business could be combined with all kinds of adventurous challenges and suddenly a number of road shows and other initiatives were mooted for other parts of the world. Inspiring people was in.

A few eyebrows were raised and I suspect that, had I been reporting to one or two middle managers at the time, I might have been in trouble, but our senior executives were very positive.

I was told later by a board member that 'we had done the right thing' and had created significant awareness for the opportunities in Africa. I felt proud to be working for a corporation, which was so open to new ideas and was willing to accept the controlled risk-taking that this clearly involved. In addition, in the end I managed to find the missing budget from my internal network.

"There's a chance I might need to ask for forgiveness….."

The real consequences of the last few years of frenetic activity were however personal. As mentioned, we had planned to walk the South Downs Way on my return and this was indeed an ideal way of de-stressing. We were three couples, Agata and I, Terrence and Joanne and James and Zoe and, after a pleasant week and a hundred miles or so of walking, we finished near Eastbourne.

It was shortly after this that Agata told me she wanted a divorce. My long absences had no doubt been a factor, but we had grown apart and she was determined to start a new life. There was, and had been, no one else involved, just an inevitability, which I was forced to accept.

There was no real hostility. We decided that we would wait for Agata to secure a full time job contract before telling Katie, or before one of us moved out. In reality, this meant living in the same house for another year. We remained on reasonable terms during this period and were able to agree on all the important things. I insisted on co-parenting for Katie – a very Dutch approach, where the child spends alternate weeks with each parent, who share the costs. I would also remain in the house, as Agata could not afford the mortgage by herself.

At work, my boss passed me a message with a smile. "No more big initiatives this year…. why not take some holiday?" All of this led to a quiet thoughtful autumn.

By Christmas, Radhika and I were determined to do a second 'Cape to Cairo' roadshow in 2011 and started planning and lobbying. It was during this process that I was approached with a new challenge.

It was clear that our business would be renewing its focus on Africa and the local management wanted a selected group of thirteen so called 'high potentials' from the continent to come together to create new business ideas and an overall plan. Did I have any ideas?

I mulled it over for a few days. Traditional doctrine said you went to a hotel somewhere, locked yourselves away and turned your mobiles off for a week. Surely, we could do better. I instinctively sensed a new opportunity to combine climbing with business.

Slowly the core of an idea emerged. What if we took the team to Zermatt for the week and rented self-catering apartments with views of the Matterhorn?

We would create a program to acclimatize and prepare the group, in between and after working sessions, for a team ascent of the Breithorn (4164 m).

Would this combination of inspiring surroundings, a relaxed but tough working schedule and a seemingly impossible challenge/shared experience create exciting new ideas? From

Zermatt the north face of the Breithorn looks rather imposing to the un-initiated although the summit can be reached quite easily by Alpine standards from the direction of the Kleine Matterhorn cable car station some three hundred and sixty metres below the peak.

Could I sell this one? Again, I needed to find the person who could say yes!

There was indeed only one way to find out and I submitted a detailed proposal, with a budget of twenty thousand euros excluding travel. This might seem a lot, but in the world of corporate consultancy, it is not.

The answer indeed turned out to be 'yes.'

The response from our African management team was enthusiastic, extremely enthusiastic in fact. Plans were made with support by our Human Resources team to ensure the right people, with the right visas, would be on location at the right time.

We moved quickly. I contacted the Zermatt tourist office, who referred me to a very competent local organizer, a young lad who was an accomplished mountaineer himself. He quickly entered into the spirit of things and organized a couple of self-catering apartments – separate for men and women but with one large communal area with a balcony, overlooking the Matterhorn.

The Zermatt team developed a program of acclimatization for the week and reserved some of the best guides in Zermatt, for the west summit of the Breithorn. We would of course be doing the standard hike up from the Klein Matterhorn.

The full itinerary was developed and timed for late June 2011. We would either be working or acclimatizing for the ascent, arriving Sunday afternoon and starting Sunday evening.

Each day we would have working sessions plus an activity. It all seemed straightforward. We just needed good weather for the end of the week.

We would be fifteen people – my Dutch boss, known to all as DP and I would facilitate the working side, whilst the local Zermatt team would manage the acclimatization, the safety elements and the climb. This was the plan in its simplest form.

Our team members flew in from South Africa, Egypt and Morocco. We all arrived within hours at Zermatt's railway terminus and I began to sense how special a trip this was for many.

There were many amazed expressions. I already knew that some of my colleagues, smart, university educated, had never experienced snow before, but many of them also remarked that they had never seen trees growing on the side of hills.

We were a mixture of ages, mostly young, with different faiths, cultures, backgrounds and tastes in music, but despite this, there was a very positive atmosphere from the start.

The surroundings were inspiring and the relaxed, informal atmosphere helped facilitate matters. Everyone was motivated and professional and we all instinctively felt 'the opportunity to make a difference.'

The next week was a busy one. Either we worked, or cooked or walked up paths, gaining height as the week went by. The first evening we hiked from Zermatt up to the Edelweiss café. (1970m) we then spent a night sleeping at the Fluhalp hut 2606 m, before returning early the next day to the valley and our work the following morning.

There were sessions with crampons and we spent a couple of hours one afternoon up at the Klein Matterhorn region (3800 m) walking roped-up to the Italian frontier. Team Zermatt certainly knew their business.

There was no nightlife in the town for us. It was not banned; we simply did not feel the need. Meals were prepared together in our apartments and the chores shared. We discovered a shared sense of humour (people really are the same) and laughter was present. Sleep was appreciated after the long days, and we operated an 'early to bed, early to rise' routine.

In between all this, we worked very hard. New ideas were discussed and developed or rejected. We had the usual breakout sessions, and small, group-analysis of issues. Inspiration was always close to hand; our balconies overlooked the Matterhorn, the sun shone a lot of the time and I noticed many smiling glances out.

This view of Switzerland's most famous mountain certainly seemed to work. One of the ideas we discussed and developed would prove an important part of my life for the next few years. Everyone was aware of the solar powered lighting of small, football pitches, which we had developed for the first 'Cape to Cairo' roadshow. These had been temporary solutions, which we took away with us after the games.

However, what if we installed fixed solar-powered area lighting solutions and built up activities around them? Could this help enable social and economic development in communities, which lived off-grid, by providing security and extending their day. Could we offer this as a business proposition and what other spins-offs could it generate?

Collectively we drew up the blue prints for what we called a 'Community Light Centre' or CLC for short. Our experience had been that 1000 square metres was sufficient an area to light for either sport or social events. Nor did it need to be too bright. There would anyway be a balance between amount of light and cost.

Discussions took place on such questions as ownership, warranty, replacement policy, supply-chain, marketing, and pricing, the potential for vandalism and theft, impact-research and, not least, the best places to build the sites. Another debate I remember was on which partners we could and should approach, to develop this further, on the accepted basis that developing new ideas anywhere was always going to require alliances and partnerships to succeed. Our conclusions were recorded.

Whilst the Matterhorn was a distant inspiration we were also aware that the Breithorn was going to be a reality and for most the view of the North-face when viewed from Zermatt, was daunting. I had explained that this was a metaphor for our business experience, and that what seemed very difficult would actually turn out to be very achievable, if you followed the right path.
I had long noticed that people living on the African continent whether from the Mediterranean north or the sub-Saharan middle and south are mentally very tough. Their lives are lived, mostly without the same safety nets as Europe and they are willing to take greater risks. They also seemed to have confidence in what I was telling them.

We had aimed for a Friday morning ascent and the weather obliged us. Only one of our party would not be going, due to an old knee injury. At our early breakfast, I could see the sense of anticipation on all the faces.
We set off before dawn to the cable car station and were on the first lifts up. Our guides looked tough and competent and seemed slightly bemused at being hired for what to them was no more than a simple walk on the glacier.
The dawn looked great with clear views all round and it promised to be a perfect day. We were reasonably well acclimatized, well equipped and in the best of hands.
Yet I was conscious of feeling slightly tense, something which I had never felt on the Breithorn before. When we arrived at the Klein Matterhorn, we sat down in the restaurant area and had a drink and a final toilet stop. 'A nice touch this' I thought which I

would recommend. Most of the parties with us went straight out onto the snow and started roping up.

We set ourselves up soon enough with two ropes of seven. The route was very familiar – down and out across the glacier, gently heading up towards the final, steeper slopes. We made good progress and rested as usual just before the bergschrund. It was a perfect day and there were few people about.

There was quite a bit of banter and faces were smiling. This was indeed proving a lot easier than they might have feared and I noticed my tension had disappeared.

About forty-five mins later, we summited together at 4164 m. The view was clear and our group energy levels were high. A number of flags appeared, including our company colours and a few national ones and everyone gathered and sang for the summit team-photo.

The summit is what the Breithorn really does well. There are views to die for, a nice, flat non-threatening space to stand or sit and a sense, for the non-mountaineer, that they have climbed Everest. It is something inspiring, to remember for the rest of your life.

We did not stay long though. It was bitterly cold and a few people quickly started complaining about their hands and faces. We were soon racing down the slopes and on the seemingly long walk back to the Klein Matterhorn.

There was no lingering and were soon back on the cable car heading down. Crammed in, I remember standing next to my manager DP, who was furiously checking his mobile phone for emails and missing as I thought a great close-up view of the Breithorn North Face.

When I pointed this out, he turned half smiling and said 'I haven't told you before but I have a fear of heights'. Without letting on or showing it, and for the sake of his team, he had been suffering all morning; a good manager indeed.

Shortly afterwards we said our thanks and good-byes to the climbing guides and the rest of the local Swiss team. A few of the guides seemed bemused. Used to clients settling for nothing less than a major route, they were slowly adjusting to our lesser demands, and lower satisfaction threshold.

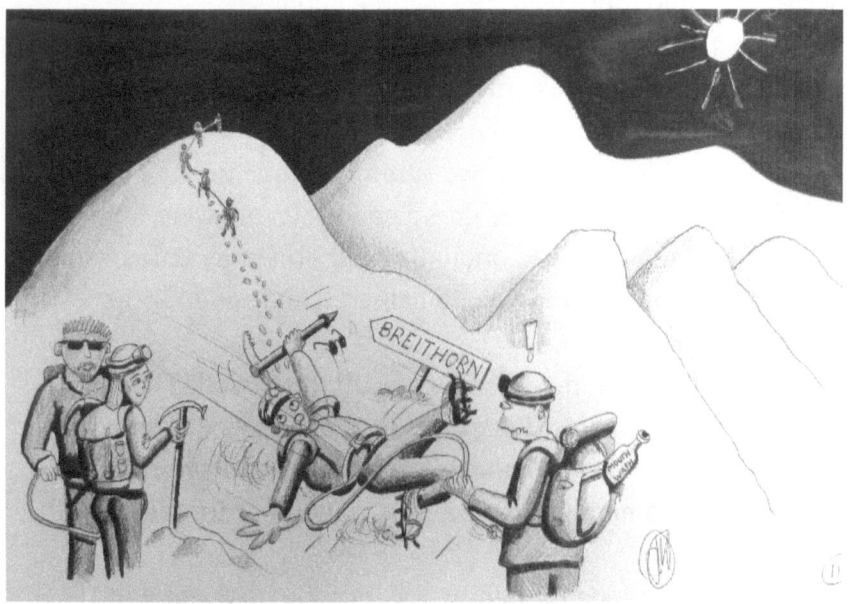

Humour is universal!

We returned, contented and smiling, to our apartments in Zermatt, showered and lunched and then settled down to an afternoon's work. Our plan needed finishing and this was the moment of maximum inspiration.

So how much did this 'moment' and indeed the whole week impact upon the quality of our work? After all, this was one of the key criteria for the week. My answer is a subjective yes and my case as follows.

People were genuinely inspired – there is no doubt about that.

They told us at the time and I witnessed it too. They also said so afterwards in a survey. Nor should this be surprising as, to witness snow covered peaks and valleys of trees for the first time, is surely memorable. To stand on top of a 4000 m peak, even if only partly by your own efforts, is also something you will remember. The team's mind-set was very much about teamwork and cooperation from the start as if awed by the whole undertaking.

Differences in culture, language, and religion became invisible and people mixed effectively. I do not remember a harsh word spoken all week and we mostly came from hard worlds and were used to all kinds of conflicts.

Did all this create inspiring ideas? This is the crux, and here is where my subjectivity comes in. We did create new ideas and at least two were to be adopted by our company. I cannot go into details due to company confidentiality, but the frame of 'mind stretching' we induced was optimal to thinking 'outside the box.'

Would we have had the same impact had we been conventional, gone to a run of the mill hotel, and locked ourselves in? I cannot prove it, but I doubt it. Moreover, I would wager that today, more than five years later, people would remember this week and the points we discussed, far more than any number of conventional meetings.

They will also remember the brand name that enabled them to do so. Such is the power of mountains.

To further back this up I can also point, in hindsight, to a very high retention rate amongst those present for quite a number of years afterwards and the feeling of a shared bond, when further meetings took place. In short, I felt and still feel we had succeeded all round.

We finally finished our plan by early evening and allowed ourselves some time in town, for the first time that week. It was our last night together, as we would all be heading home on the Saturday morning.

We had brought Africa to Zermatt that week in what I would guess was a unique, if tiny insignificant way in the grand scheme of things. Yet in a few hundred million years, Africa will be calling again, literally and physically as its northern tectonic plate will push the Alps up to heights beyond the Himalayas today. I smiled at the idea we might have left a very, very, early calling card!

Afterwards I had one more thought. Could this approach work as an exclusive business model for corporations and other large organizations? Yes, almost certainly I concluded, although to this date I have not found the time to follow this up.

2011 remained a busy year. In May, I had been rock-climbing in Belgium for a few days with Mark for the first time in several years. It was here that we learned of the death of Bin Laden in a US raid.

I would climb the Breithorn two more times that summer, and this had now become a standard joke amongst my friends.

The second time was in July, along with friends including JR and Jane, and as part of a three-week 'father/daughter only holiday' with Katie.

Incidentally, we walked on Mont Blanc too, went on a cruise and finished off with a low cost wet week in an outward-bound centre in South Wales with more friends. Katie would remember this week as the best. Clearly, throwing money at holidays is not the answer.

The third time was in early September when I went again to Zermatt, as part of a four day, round-trip with a small group of senior company managers. We drove from the Netherlands. The weather remained kind and we summited the Breithorn again without any difficulties.

In between and around all this Radhika and I fitted in another 'Cape to Cairo' road show, although not on the scale of the year before. We drove a branded vehicle with some colleagues from Cape Town along the coast to Durban and then up to Johannesburg. We subsequently completed events too, in Nairobi, Abuja (Nigeria) and Cairo. It was a lot less stressful than the year before.

In October, my divorce came through and we adopted the Dutch shared parenting approach. Agata, who could not afford our mortgage by herself, had moved to a house just around the corner and Katie would spend alternate weeks with me. I tried to plan my travels around this and mostly succeeded.
I was also keen that she would learn something about her British roots and we often went for a weekend to London or Brighton, staying with family and friends. We could go out on Friday afternoon after school, via Calais and sometimes be in South London before 2100. This approach proved very successful with the only costs being a tank of petrol and a low cost ferry ticket.

At work, we were soon planning again and I was determined to include the mountains in these considerations. The Alps had proved their business-worth in Europe, at least to my immediate management, and me but they were not practical for our local teams in Africa to travel to.
The obvious thing would be to utilize the famous peaks of Africa in the future. This got me thinking again.

Above: 2012 Playing 'Winston' at John and Jane's wedding at Ironbridge Shropshire

Below: 2011 walking with Katie on the lower slopes of Mont Blanc

Above: Team Africa at dinner in Zermatt 2011. I spent the week with some great Egyptian, Moroccan and South African colleagues.

Below: Setting of for the Breithorn 2011

Above and below: We trained and acclimatized after our working sessions – near Zermatt 2011

Above: A view to inspire. Taken from our balcony where we worked during the day.

Below: Testing our gear and ourselves. For some this was their first ever experience of snow and ice.

Above: On the summit of the Breithorn at 4164m

Below: I simply like Zermatt.

6. Mountaineering and Marketing. 2012-13

By the start of 2012, I had become a single parent and father to a beautiful, eleven year old daughter who was growing up fast. I was supported by my parents and Annetta and her family, who all lived conveniently nearby, and together we managed to avoid any situations, which left Katie home alone.

That March saw my fiftieth birthday. Katie and I travelled over to the UK to Brighton, where James and Zoe had organized a venue and a band composed of some of James's friends. Team ID were invited and turned up in large numbers. We billed it as the 'Kelso hundred party' with Katie and me at fifty, Will at forty at ten!

The music was very sixties at my special request.

By now, I was noticeably slowing down and gaining weight all too easily. Dieting and training left only small dents in what was becoming more than just, a little 'middle-age spread' and this would in due course become a serious hindrance to outdoor activities. These activities were still present and centered on family and friends.

For example that spring our immediate family (Mum, Dad, Annetta, Simon, Sean Jack, Robert, Katie and I) travelled to Carlisle to walk the Hadrian's Wall trail. James and Zoe, Roger and son James joined us and we had pre-booked our accommodation.

Our schedule was somewhat complicated – as some would be through-walkers and do the whole thing, whilst others 'in support' and 'in cars' would walk the best bits only! Having done the trail twice I had a clear recollection of 'the best bits' and as Katie and I would be day walkers. It also meant my stamina was not tested that week, as we walked no more than half the route.

The 'through walkers', Annetta, Jack aged ten, Roger and son James arrived at Wallsend, having completed the course, and I recall that Roger's feet looked fairly gruesome by then. It was an energizing week, something I can recommend for an active family.

We also celebrated a team ID wedding in June. JR and Jane were going to 'tie the knot' in unconventional fashion. They had hired a wedding hall at the Blists Hill, Victorian town in Ironbridge, Shropshire that appealed to both JR and Jane, as the birthplace of the Industrial Revolution.

There was a late 19th century Britain theme on site and all guests were to come in fancy dress from the period. More unconventionality followed, with JR having three 'best men', James, Jerry and me, for as he said – we had spent most of the 1990's roped together in the mountains.

The three best men were 'roped together'!

I chose to go as 'Winston Churchill', which was following up on a hunch I had had for some time. Ever since my twenties, people had been remarking, that I looked "a lot like" young Winston himself. With weight gain, this likeness had increased and it seemed an obvious choice to come dressed as him. Churchill had been born into the Victorian era, and this is how I justified the wedding theme, although I chose the 'classic 1940 look' with striped suit and cigar.

For many months I had studied his looks and voice and had scoured the retailers in the Netherlands for clothes and other 'trademark' items. This had produced good results and I was satisfied with the finished look. I received an enthusiastic reception, but the real winners were JR and Jane, who laid on a simply superb wedding.

In between all this, we had been preparing for a new 'Cape to Cairo' road show. The route would be north-west-east-south, starting in May in Cairo and arriving in Cape Town by August. It would not be overland this time. For the first time a number of company board members would attend.

We had a budget for just a handful of the so-called 'Community Light Centre's' and decided the best way to gain internal attention would be in Cairo at the start. Our local Egyptian team found an orphanage just outside the city with a football field and we installed our solar-powered floodlights and organized an event.

The impact of allowing kids to play in the evening, in a way that had never been possible before was a powerful one and we had an enthusiastic response from a number of important internal stakeholders.

Feeling encouraged, I submitted a proposal to our executive for a hundred such sites across the continent to be part of a corporate social responsibility campaign. This ticked all our 'brand-boxes' and could be linked quite easily to football. With this in mind, I went to see the Dutch Football Association - the KNVB, and met their CSR manager, who was very enthusiastic about the whole idea. The KNVB knew Africa well, and had a very wide network of contacts. The link between football and politicians and executives was also very prevalent.

Together, we developed a joint proposal and I secured some internal funding.

These joint proposals were all accepted and we signed a memorandum of understanding for three years with the KNVB, in August. By then, we had more experience from Ghana, Nigeria and Kenya, to back up what we already knew. In Nigeria, incidentally I managed to arrange with a distributor to go and see my birthplace in Ibadan, a city about three hours' drive north of Lagos.

The old nursing home as it was called back then was still there and I was able to visit the main offices where we had a chat with the local doctors. They still had the visitor records book for 1962 and I was pleased to note that today, the 'New Hospital' as it is now known is being used by local patients – as my mother had said it had seemed almost empty at the time of my birth. Based on my photos she also confirmed that the building still looked identical to 1962.

So, taken together, our vision to enable social and economic development, using solar power and LED lighting; a plan for a hundred Community Light Centre's, the 'Cape to Cairo' roadshow, our partnership with the KNVB and a renewed focus on Africa, all meant that the pieces were coming together for a big year in 2013.

Instinctively I was determined to add mountaineering to the mix. But what would be the best way to approach this? I knew from experience that a mountain challenge could engage employees, create publicity and add another human element, to what we were trying to do. I also remembered the extraordinary response from our mostly young, Egypt-team a year or two earlier, when I had told them in a formal presentation, the story of my early attempts on the Matterhorn with Tony and Terrence. (As told in the 'Alpine Game.') During the first attempt we had not worked together and had failed, whilst in the second, a couple of years later, we had worked well as a team and had succeeded.

People had suddenly 'come alive' and enthusiastic colleagues, all sharing anecdotes or ideas surrounded me. My message had been about the benefits of teamwork, but it was their passion I remembered.

What if we could get this energy and enthusiasm channeled into climbing the highest or most iconic mountain in say the north, middle and south of Africa? Moreover, by publicizing this internally and externally, we could touch upon a whole range of areas; from employee motivation, team building, and communication of key marketing messages about improving people's lives with new technology, management agendas and just showing what a cool brand we were working for.

Two events reinforced this thinking. A couple of colleagues from our corporate legal team approached me with their intent to organize a Kilimanjaro climb, and asked me for advice. I ascertained that they would be willing to expand their trip, to include representatives from the KNVB and link it to our road show, by raising funds for a Community Light Center in Tanzania.

They were young and enthusiastic.

The second was a request from the management of our North West Africa team, based in Casablanca, Morocco. They were looking for a serious, team-building event, which would help bond their young team together.

Here I remembered that a few years earlier I had proposed a team climb of Jebel Toubkal in the Atlas Mountains and at 4167 m the highest mountain in North Africa. At the time, our management had been in transition and the proposal had not been followed up.

Both of these developments helped clarify my thinking. I would approach our management teams in the various regions to gain their support. Together, we would propose a team-climb in South Africa of Table Mountain in Cape Town, which was obviously not the highest but probably the best-known and most iconic hill in the region.

This would be a straightforward proposition for our Southern Africa team, which could be completed in a half a day and would be both a team-building and promotional event.

For Central Africa, we would build on the Kilimanjaro proposal from my legal colleagues. This would be a joint approach, with our partners at the KNVB and would link directly into our Community Light Centre program.

We would install a Community Light Centre in a Tanzanian community near Arusha, and the funding would be raised via the team. The team would do the climb, at own expense and in their own time.

For North Africa, I updated and resubmitted the idea, for a group ascent of Jebel Toubkal. Although listed as a trekking peak, with no technical climbing (on the standard route) I stressed this should be on a voluntary basis only, with those not willing to undertake this being allowed to cheer people on from the sidelines.

I also pointed out the need for medical checks and guides with full, logistical support. The business angle would be the promotion of our 'Cape to Cairo' roadshow and team building. To my surprise, not only was the proposal accepted, but also with only one or two exceptions, the forty-five person team signed up for the enterprise.

About half were young women, about whom a lot more in this

chapter. Such was the enthusiasm that I did not need to organize a thing. Within a few weeks, they had sorted out the whole adventure, via a local trekking company. Equally satisfying was the fact that they had invited me to come along with them!

The date was set for late August 2013 and I booked my flights. All these proposals were accepted, and were included in our planning. There had been no opposition or dissent, and the general reaction of my Egyptian colleagues had been repeated across the continent.

I was invited to join the Table Mountain team in Cape Town in May, which boosted my own commitment to our work!

Most of this planning took place in the winter of 2012/13. I knew at the time that my mind was writing cheques my body had no way of cashing. My weight gain had reached record levels and my fitness was such that I would find a minor Lakeland hill challenging, let alone the highest that North Africa had to offer.

Therefore, I would have to start 2013 by dieting in a serious way. I knew I would need to lose at least fifteen kg and do a lot of training by August to stand a chance of summiting in Morocco.

In fact, as chance would have it, we spent a family Christmas 2012 in the Lake District, and I did struggle on some of the minor hills and mostly in the rain of course!

During this period, Katie and I regularly spent either weekends in London, staying with my brother Will or other friends. It was a good way of staying in touch with our roots and enhancing Katie's education.

During this period, I must have dragged Katie around just about every Winston Churchill monument or museum in the south of England. I was also still occasionally giving battlefield tours at weekends, to groups from the British army or local contacts.

My diet progressed well and by April, I had lost about eight kg. That month we had a family holiday with my parents in Shropshire, hiring a longboat on the canals and somehow managing to avoid sinking or crashing into anything large for four days. Again, I would highly recommend this sort of activity to active family groups.

May in Cape Town, saw the start of our 2013 Cape to Cairo roadshow. Our friends at the KNVB joined us too. They had brought some high profile, former international footballers from across Africa and the Netherlands. These were a great bunch of people, who played against the local kids at a football ground, lit by our solar powered lights, on the slopes below Table Mountain. It was a magical setting.

Our local South African team set out to climb Table Mountain. We were about ten managers, led by an excellent, young German called Mark.

The team was mostly young and fit, as South Africans generally are, and we had hired a guide to point us up the right path. There are several routes up this iconic hill and we chose a good one up the south-ocean side.

This reminded me of the Breithorn, as viewed from Zermatt, because it looked impossible from below. However, the path snaked its way up between a crack in the rock structure high up and emerged onto the summit area.

We set off in the morning and it only took a few hours to get to the top. I was conscious of some of the younger members, looking at me quizzically as if thinking 'is he going to make it' as I was still well overweight. I had the same thoughts myself but I managed it, at a slow pace, bringing up the rear but not embarrassingly so.

On the summit, we had a clear view of the ocean and hills around. It was a stunning setting of the sun. I remember watching that day as this group of managers came together, and grew as a team. This experience, whilst hardly very challenging, was so unusual and unexpected in their daily lives that it could not but enthuse and unite.

A few of us stayed on for the weekend and went shark diving at our own expense. I remember touching a six foot, 'Great White' as it slithered past my cage somewhere off the tip of the continent. South Africa is simply unique.

This was in May and by August, we had a great many more memories; the giraffe that had joined our media briefing outdoors in a tent near Johannesburg. The massive event in the Mathare slum of Nairobi with the local governor taking penalties under our lights; the times in Accra and Lagos when we had three, ex-international football captains playing together against the local kids. At times, it seemed like one big celebration, but the passion and excitement were real and confirmed our thinking.

The second climb of the year had also gone well. In July, our joint Kilimanjaro teams had made the summit and descended, just in time to take part in an opening ceremony at a rural village site just south of Arusha in Tanzania.

I had travelled here overland from Nairobi with the KNVB and remembered seeing the fatigue on the faces of the summit party. They had also clearly bonded, but I was aware that I could not have climbed with them in my current state. It remained to be seen if I could lose enough weight to make Jebel Toubkal feasible.

Just to make things more challenging, we had organized an all-inclusive Mediterranean cruise in early August, with Terrence and his daughters and Annetta, Simon and their kids. By force-of- will, I managed to lose half a kg that week, using the gym facilities a lot and only having a few beers a night.

That summer I was also lucky enough to witness another one of Africa's finest cultural experiences - a traditional Zulu wedding.

A Dutch friend and colleague called Henk, had moved to South Africa and was set to marry a local girl called Joy. The wedding would be a traditional one in Natal and I had been invited, along with a Hungarian friend.

We hired a car in Johannesburg for the weekend and drove down via Durban to the remote rural setting on a hill with a great view of the Indian Ocean. There on the hillside, the marriage ceremony took place amidst the dancing, singing, traditional costumes, spears, and the sacrifice of a couple of cows. The Zulus certainly are a formidable people.

And so on to late August in Morocco and Jebel Toubkal. Despite having shed some fifteen kg since January, I knew it would be a brutal slog and that I would have to rely a good deal on will power.

I travelled from Brussels with Air Morocco. This was usually an interesting flight. Amongst other things, I had once experienced an upgrade to business class, for the first and only time in my life, only to end up in the middle of a fistfight between two businessmen, who were sitting next to me.

These two took exception to each other somewhere over the Mediterranean. The cabin crews were excellent. We got free drinks, another story to tell, and the police were waiting for my neighbours after landing.

At our company offices in Casablanca, there was a palpable sense of excitement and anticipation. The normally clean rooms and hallways were strewn with rucksacks and gear and our teams were huddled in groups, chatting in hushed tones. There had been a massive buy-in and involvement for the idea, for although the trip was not compulsory, only one person out of forty-six was not coming.

The number of young women involved also struck me, roughly about half of the total group. Many had back-office business support functions so I would not normally have met them, but their enthusiasm for our adventure was striking.

A staff committee had worked out all the details including hiring in a specialist guiding company and everything ran efficiently. We left in several coaches just after midday and drove across to Marrakech, and then on to Imlil (1740 m) at the start of the climb.

It was summer and the temperatures in the valley had just peaked at 50C a few days before. The views were great and I was reminded that Winston Churchill had once described this area in 1943, as the 'nicest place on earth to spend an afternoon.' I can appreciate his point, but suspect it was not close to 50C at the time of his visit, that his main reference was wartime Britain and he was well supplied with his favorite drinks!

On arrival, we loaded our rucksacks onto donkeys and set out for an easy, hour's walk up the valley to our first overnight stop. This was in a small village, clinging to the side of the hills, where we had an excellent meal on a terrace, high up overlooking a river.

After this, there was strict segregation. The men went one way to some basic dormitories and the women the other way to their own accommodation. It was clear the local culture was very self-regulating in this regard.

We set off early after breakfast and before the sun rose. It was a fascinating, scenic, and ultimately exhausting day. We were heading up to the Toubkal hut some ten km up the valley. On paper in guidebooks, this is seen as a short walk-in – some five hours and almost irrelevant to the real business, which commences the next day.

I can now caution against this view! It was a tough fifteen hundred metre ascent up to the Toubkal hut at 3206 m, relentless, almost barren and very hot. The only oasis, and it is a spectacular one, is about half way up where the valley bends to the east past the tiny settlement of Sidi Chamharouch.

My lack of fitness condemned me to drop back slowly but surely until I was walking with the stragglers. This also allowed me to witness the way our group dealt with the climb. Despite the warnings to take it easy, most of the young men simply raced on ahead and disappeared from view quickly.

Most of the women split into groups, self-contained and self-supporting, moving at their own pace. A few, with good negotiating skills, managed to commandeer rides up on the numerous donkeys, which accompanied our rucksacks and us. At the rear, we also formed a group and I pretended I saw my role as supporting and motivating this group to keep going.

After Sidi Chamharouch, the path lead over a stream and ran steeply uphill to the right side of the Isougouane valley, which led finally, and after many hours of sweat, to two stone-built refuges (The old Neltner Refuge and the new Refuge du Toubkal). By the time we in the last group arrived, it was already mid-afternoon and we had been on the go for about eight hours.

A drink, a late lunch and a rest later, I was able to take notes. Our whole team of forty-five had made it, which was a triumph in itself.

The main open question that pre-occupied everyone was – who wanted to go for the summit the next morning? Our guides appeared happy for us to decide, although they would have known this process was mostly self-regulating, as most instinctively already knew the answer.

A few, particularly the women, had lively debates in public and sought confirmation from their friends, or so I was told, as most of the talk was in Arabic. I was struck by the determination of many, who had clearly had a tough day, to continue.

The new Toubkal hut was modern, attractive and comforting with good facilities. We rested, chatted, smiled and dined together. Finally, there were about thirty confirmations for the summit push and the guides decided to split us into three groups. I was happy to join Eric, our General Manager, in the last group, which mostly consisted of young women. It was to be an instructive choice.

Just after 21.00 that evening, we went to our strictly segregated dormitories. Sleep was short, breakfast was early and we set out at 03.00. The ascent was about a thousand metres and should take about five hours.

In the dark, the route seemed straightforward enough and a steady procession of head-torches made its way up. Here and there were some rock steps, which required some hands on scrambling but nothing worrying.

I soon began to notice the young women in our group were constantly asking their friends how they were, and encouraging each other. I think that for all of them it was a unique experience of freedom in a strange and challenging environment. None of them seemed physically very fit, yet they adopted a comfortable pace and were happy to go with the slowest.

I thanked my lucky stars, as I knew this was my only chance of getting to the top.

Three hours later, it began to get light, and we stopped to rest. Some of the young men, who had gone on ahead in the lead group, came back past us. They looked exhausted and reported that they had turned round and just wanted to sleep.

The first all-male group had apparently set out to race up the mountain and the pace had broken quite a few of them. Shortly after, a few more came by reporting the same thing.

After daylight, the difference in approach between the men and women became even clearer. We continued up at the pace of the slowest, and stopped frequently for those who needed to rest.

There was no tension and it seemed they had instinctively decided not to leave anyone behind. Shouts of encouragement mixed with laughter, jokes and even a bit of singing.

My own mind felt numb, as I took this all in and continued to bring up the rear. In reality, I was hanging on grimly, a bit like a 'Tour de France' cyclist bringing up the rear in the mountains and hoping to make the time limit cut.

Despite our stops becoming more frequent, we made steady progress and could now see the summit area. There was no snow, just rocky, easy-angled slopes and it reminded me of the upper slopes of Kilimanjaro just before Gilman's point. At this stage, we met the first group coming down. About half a dozen of them had made the summit in fine time and they were pleased.

They said the second group, which was mostly male but which had some of the strongest women too, had been approaching the top when they had left. I watched them disappear down the mountainside in the same style as they had climbed up it, namely far too fast for me!

"So I tagged along at the back to witness the teamwork….."

About an hour later, we met the second group returning from the summit, or should I say just over half the second group for they too had 'lost' a number of colleagues on the way up.

By this, stage my pretense to be guarding the rear of the group had disappeared, as I started to fall behind even the slowest of our group. At first, the gap was just a few metres, but it grew with time to about ten minutes.

However, they knew where I was and were waiting for me at the summit. The views were three hundred and sixty degrees and spectacular. Our entire group of ten had made it and we smiled for the photos.

It was only afterwards that I realized the significance of this. These young women had never climbed a mountain before. They were not physically very strong; knew very little about acclimatization and had little or no experience to fall back on. They had not been the quickest, yet they had all made the summit together, and had the highest success rate amongst the teams. Instinctively they had worked together as a team. They had supported each other throughout; kept up their own spirits during the tough moments, and encouraged and inspired each other.

I would still wager a large bet today, that had they been alone, virtually none of them would have succeeded.

Moreover, there was another point. These young women were all mentally incredibly strong and determined. I have already referred to this observation before and today cannot help wondering how many people from a randomly chosen, European office could come close to this strength of mind.

Their capacity to absorb pain, exhaustion, heat or cold, whilst dealing with the unknown was remarkable.

These thoughts of course only occurred much later, for at the time my mind was on autopilot. I merely felt a vague sense of relief that we had succeeded so far in our aim. Some twenty-one people had made the summit of North Africa.

It was about 08.00 and we had a dinner appointment arranged in Marrakech that evening.

Our descent to the hut was uneventful and we arrived back just before midday. Most of the group had already set off for the valley and our guides allowed us an hour. I spent most of this time asleep whilst the others ate.

The slog down the valley is a hazy memory, and sometime after Sidi Chamharouch, I lost touch with the group and found myself alone, accompanied only by a couple of climbing guides.

I felt embarrassed but try as I might, I could not re-connect with them. Then after about an hour, I came across a man with a donkey. He gestured that I should climb on its back. I waivered but the climbing guides explained that the others had all done the same, and were now donkey-bound for the valley.

This certainly speeded things up but my guides got too far ahead and my donkey-guide lost his way – so we spent about 2 hours wandering along small, steep paths with huge, vertical-drops. I was quite conscious that any stumble from my animal and I would have been lost – and I can tell you it was carrying a substantial weight.

I amused myself by thinking what our health and safety people might have had to say.

By the time we reached the valley, the others had long gone in the coaches, leaving a message of encouragement. Some of the climbing guides with a van gave me a lift to Marrakech – about an hour's drive to the north and dropped me at our hotel.

After an unusually long shower and change of clothes, I made my way to the restaurant for our company meal. For some reason my tiredness had by now vanished. Marrakech is a magical place.

The next morning the team posed for another group photo. Spirits were very high, and even those who had not made the summit, looked relaxed. In this respect, it appeared we had succeeded in strengthening the sense of a team.

Certainly, the HR manager, who had not made the summit, seemed to think so. Time will tell in this case. Today I remember a remarkable group of people, who are building a business and a brand and wish them well.

That autumn I wrote up reports and conclusions on what had been a remarkable summer. This account has focused on the integration of mountaineering into our program, but I think some *perspective* on the impact and investment in this 'Mountaineering and Marketing' approach is important. To help provide this sense of proportion, I can state that all our climbs from Table Mountain, Kilimanjaro and Jebel Toubkal amounted to just one slide with conclusions in the final presentation.

In this case, they did not *directly* bring in large orders, or reduce costs and enable efficiencies and all the other areas that corporations look to identify. They did on the other hand generate publicity and support our brand messaging in a positive way.

But to me they were primarily about inspiring people, and helping people come together and bond as a real team, something which often happens after sharing a tough but really meaningful experience as the military well know.

In addition, here is one final observation from the human perspective.

I will again bet anything that, for those who took part in these events, the memories and the name of the company that enabled them to do it will remain long after all the other many business initiatives we took that summer are long forgotten. Indeed, I am struggling to remember the rest of that report even now!

Looking back, I can really appreciate the progressive attitude of many of the senior managers in our corporation, who understood what we were trying to achieve and who gave it their backing, without which, it would never have happened. They were the ones who said 'yes' to the ideas.

In the previous chapters, I have given some of my experiences of how mountaineering and adventure can lead to 'win-win' scenarios in business and corporate life. The challenge needs to be realistic, whilst the risks need careful consideration and professional support.

Participation should be voluntary and each situation is different. However, it can be done and it can work.

We are all driven by emotions and passions – along with ideas they are the most powerful of things. From a corporate perspective, making money for other people is a tricky concept with which to inspire someone's soul with, however dutifully we go about it. Enabling people to express themselves and expand their horizons along the way, does help.

In fact combining your passions in life with your work, I have noted, usually means that output and impact will increase significantly.

So how much can we take from the experiences I have described? As I write in 2016, I am aware that questions have long been raised about the future of corporations, with their often dinosaur-like proportions and speed.

Evolution after all suggests 'small, fast and agile' usually lasts longer. I think the principles and benefits of 'Corporate adventure' can apply to either.

Change has been rapid in recent years. Today it is less than ten years since I wrote the Alpine Game – in a world *without* smart phones, tablets, and the internet of things, Facebook, WhatsApp, numerous medical breakthroughs, the 'Arab spring' and its consequences, and an endless list of other things.

Moreover, so much more change is still to come. Job destroying robots within a few years and predictions about how we will be able to create anything out of atoms, using super algorithms, within a hundred and fifty years raises serious questions about what we will do, as humans, by then.

'Playing games' is surely at least part of the answer.

Above: On top of Table Mountain 2013 with our South African management team.

Below: The joint summit team on Kilimanjaro 2013.

Above: Starting out on Jebel Toubkal 2013.

Below: The Toubkal hut after long climb up

Above: Early morning with the women team on Jebel Toubkal.

Below: The summit of North Africa – real teamwork 2013

Above: Donkeys were used to carry people as well as supplies

Below: A traditional Zulu wedding. Henk is on the right.

7. Ventures, health and family. 2013-2016

So what happened next? My usual answer to this question is that if you are still alive, then life goes on. The story to date is also eventful but best told briefly.

During the autumn of 2013, I developed some new corporate-social responsibility-ideas with the Dutch Football Association. Together with my contact Johan, we planned for an Africa Solar Soccer Cup for young people.

The idea was to promote our new solar lighting by sponsoring an evening tournament of five a-side football teams – both boys and girls – to be played under our new solar lighting. Six countries would be invited (I forget which now) to send their 'champions' to play in the African finals in one of the largest slums of Nairobi. We would invite big name African soccer stars to participate and of course the media.

It was a simple but effective idea and by November 2013, I had secured the budget for it. Then something happened which put all this on hold.

I was asked by my company to set up a new business venture to turn our outdoor-community, solar-lighting proposition into a viable business. This would in effect mean putting the Solar Cup idea on the back burner. After some thought, I agreed and spent the next eighteen months working around the clock, to get the new business off the ground.

Our proposition was the Community Light Centre (CLC), which was essentially an outdoor area of between one thousand and seven thousand square metres, floodlit to a high level using new LED lighting technology.

It ran off a centralized container-based solar-power unit and, because it allowed life in the evenings for communities living with access to electricity, we positioned it as enabling both social and economic development. I was particularly keen to light the slums of Nairobi in this way. In fact, it was the culmination of the ideas we had been developing since 2009. Deciding to focus on two countries only, I selected Kenya and Nigeria and recruited an excellent team in both.

In practice, I was responsible for everything from our team; product development and sourcing; logistics, sales; marketing; legal matters and, of course the all-important bottom line.

For a while, I was on a mission.

We worked with existing partners, such as the Dutch Football Association and with the UN. I was invited to talk at an UNIDO (United Nations Industrial Development Organization) summit in Vienna on our project, and addressed one of the largest audiences I had ever faced.

We had meetings with the EU in Brussels about funding for some development projects and with the Dutch Government.

I travelled regularly to Nairobi and Lagos with a few visits to Southern Africa thrown in. These involved mostly night flights, after which I would throw myself into the problems of the day. There were many issues, ranging from local suppliers and contractors to import duties and our own corporate processes, which were not designed for small start-ups.

It was also dangerous work. A colleague I had just briefed in Lagos was kidnapped and murdered a few weeks later whilst a member of my team whom I had just appointed was robbed twice at gunpoint.

We were also spending a lot of time, without bodyguards, in some of the worst slums in Africa, where violence was a way of life and people were always on the 'front line.'

On the home front, I managed to plan my trips to keep looking after Katie for one week in every two. She was now going to the local International school and starting to enjoy herself there. I was also still fitting in some weekend battlefield-tours at

Arnhem and a number of lecture events around Winston Churchill.

In February 2014, a new woman entered my life. Dimphy was Dutch with three grown-up daughters and four very young granddaughters. She lived nearby and my weekends consequently became even busier.

That summer we had a week in Northern England and a four-day trip to Zermatt, sleeping in the car on the way and climbing the Oberrothorn and the Breithorn.

All this helped cement our relationship and in January 2015 Dimphy moved in to live with Katie and myself.

People from all sides liked the Community Light Centre business proposition. Slowly our sales funnel, as it is called, developed and we started to see the first orders coming in. Life meanwhile continued at a hundred miles per hour and by the middle of 2015 clear progress had been made.

Then I hit a proverbial brick wall as my health let me down.

I had for a few months before, started to feel very tired in the mornings and had found myself less and less productive at work. I had also experienced significant weight gain, without a real change in diet, and had long lost the 2013 reductions.

By early June, matters came to a head after I was able to do no more than answer a few emails in an entire morning.

Reluctantly, though knowing something was wrong, I approached my boss, who referred me to the company doctor. She diagnosed a 'Burn Out' as the symptoms seemed to fit well including the background circumstances.

I entered a strange new world of being at home on full pay with little to do. In the meantime, my role as Venture Manager was swiftly taken over by others – proof of the old adage that nobody is indispensable!

For the first few weeks, it felt good to have a rest after almost thirty years of work. The sun shone and I watched the entire Tour de France for the first time in my life.

The doctor had advised me to be physically active and in August I just about managed to climb the Breithorn again, with Katie then aged just fourteen, Annetta and her thirteen-year-old son Jack, thus fulfilling an ambition harbored since Katie's birth. However, I had been very slow and Katie had carried my rucksack at the end.

A fine day out for some father daughter bonding!

By September, our company doctor wanted me back at work, but I was feeling if anything worse than in June. I was then sent for some hospital tests and was asked if I knew anything about sleep apnea. I did not, but would soon become very knowledgeable, as the results indicated I was suffering from the most severe-form of sleep apnea with both central and obstructive forms. My breathing stops at night had been measured at sixty-two times per hour.

This meant that every minute of every night I stopped breathing for more than ten seconds. 'You have gone very deep' said a doctor 'your body is exhausted and it will take you up to a year to recover from this.'

Apparently, 80% of sufferers are not aware they have it and I was lucky not to have suffered permanent brain damage.

At one stroke this explained 'my problem' and I was strangely relieved for some primeval reason that it was not just general 'burn out' that had caused my downfall but an identifiable physical condition.

The good news about sleep apnea is that there is an effective treatment available called CPAP.

This entails sleeping with a mask, through which air is blown to inflate your throat at night. My treatment started almost immediately and I soon got used to this inconvenience.

"It's Sleep apnea. This is how many times per hour you stopped breathing last night!"

More medical news and a wedding dominated the next six months.

During this period, my weight too had become a serious issue. I had gained twenty-five kg in weight in the previous two years, and this was now attributed directly to my sleeping condition. Dieting would not help, I was told by doctors, as the hormones, which normally kept me thin, were not working properly.

All of this led me to take a drastic decision to have gastric bypass surgery, which was covered by my medical insurance. I undertook this step successfully in April 2016.

Subsequently I have returned to weight and fitness levels I have not enjoyed since the 1980's, and can now look forward to many more Alpine adventures in the future.

Today, although still recovering, it appears my sleep apnea is almost under control, and I am left to rue another old adage – that your health is the most important thing.

Certainly looking back, I can see how my life style had become too fast and unsustainable in recent years.

The wedding came in March 2016, when Dimphy and I got married in the Netherlands. We invited about twenty-five of the UK friends over, and had a 'Best of British, Best of Dutch' fancy dress theme; at a Dutch café which itself had a British pub theme.

It was a memorable event with Dimphy's large Dutch family all in attendance. It was also a reminder that family and friends are the most important things in life – along with your health that is! Together we have fifty years of married life experience to fall back on and this will definitely be the last marriage for both of us.

Therefore, a great deal of personal happiness has followed although at the time of writing my working future is uncertain. Long absences and false starts have blighted the past twelve months, and it may be that more change is afoot. However, this does not concern me. I am not and have never been short of ideas and as my energy slowly returns, I will continue to be busy. Perhaps my next book will be called the 'Retirement Game!'

This manuscript is the third in what is, essentially a trilogy, starting with the 'Freefall Game' and the 'Alpine Game.' All of these have been written for my children and hopefully grandchildren onwards, to record life in a, for me at least 'golden period' of the late 20th and early 21st centuries, but also inspire them in their own lives.

Life is for most people, and for most of the time, a tough often-brutal thing. I have no illusions on this score, having seen so much suffering along the way.

Almost everybody who lives a full life will experience pain, suffering and sadness on a significant scale.

How we deal with this reality is an important question of people looking for guidance. I can only offer my own experiences and conclusions. The re-occurring theme in these books of 'The Game' is carefully chosen. It does not relate to life itself, which is far too deadly serious to be seen as such, but instead to some of the things we can do to make our lives feel better.

My experience is that interests, hobbies and passions - call them what you like – in my case around such things as 'skydiving, alpinism and adventure' have given my life a tremendous sense of fun and purpose.

I should add that there is of course nothing unique in all this, as most people will probably instinctively recognize. However, these are sociable, shared activities, which entail friendships and laughter; planning; training and a sense of achievement - the very things that are best about life.

It is by finding and re-finding these 'games' to play, whatever they may be, that we can enrich our lives. It has certainly helped me. They were my own personal buoyancy aid against tough times.

I have also been lucky enough to be able to use these 'games' to help shape my own life, and do many things I had never expected to do.

Finding these 'win-win scenarios in life should always involve passion and finding the person who can say 'yes' to your ideas remains excellent advice.

Above: Team ID 2013 at Agincourt – the kids came too.

Below: 2014 Dimphy on the summit of the Breithorn. 20 years before her doctor had told her she would never walk again after a car accident.

Above: Giving a talk at the the UN in Vienna. 2014

Below: Katie's first 4000m aged 14. Summer 2015.

Acknowledgements

I would like to thank those colleagues and managers who had the vision and courage to enable the activities described in this short book.

I would also like to thank my parents along with Mark Phillips, Roger Sexton and Katie Kelso for their willingness to proof read my ramblings and to suggest valuable corrections, without which this book would have been even less readable. As always a big thanks you is also due to James Hunt for his drawings and illustrations.

Finally, a big thank you to my family and particularly my children who have inspired this book more than they know and for whom, along with their own offspring, it was written in the first place.

www.ingramcontent.com/pod-product-compliance
Lightning Source LLC
Chambersburg PA
CBHW030647220526
45463CB00005B/1670